CONTENTS

£2

INTRODUCTION

INTRO
DUCTI
ON

WELCOME
TO BIBLEFRESH

Bullets tore through the air, the staccato of automatic rifle fire sounding like a thousand firecrackers being launched a few yards from our window. The night was in chaos: prisoners escaping, military arsenals rifled and happy fire lighting the air. We huddled beneath the sill and found a lifeline of hope in the words of Psalm 46 (NIV):

God is our refuge and our strength,
an ever-present help in trouble.
Therefore we will not fear, though the earth give way
and the mountains fall into the heart of the sea,
though its waters roar and foam
and the mountains quake with their surging.

As we sat in the hospital corridor coming to terms with the loss of an unborn baby, verses about the experiences of David, the emotions of Jesus and the sovereignty of God came to mind and brought us comfort.

As I left the room after a tense meeting, where tactless words were spoken, and cruel manoeuvrings that undermined the security of home, job and future were uncovered, it was the Bible that helped me keep on trusting in the overriding power and justice of God.

It is often in these difficult times that the Bible becomes most alive to us and we hear God's voice speaking directly into our lives with peace, comfort, warning and wisdom.

But God promises to speak to us whenever we read the Bible, in whatever circumstance, bad or good. This is what makes the Bible like no other book. Not just because it has been banned in more countries than any other; nor because it has been translated into more languages than any other. Not even because it would be the global best-seller every day of every year if its sales statistics were counted. And not because of its extraordinary origins, having been penned on three different continents over thousands of years, by a huge range of people in a vast array of situations: from prisoners to poets, politicians to prophets, tax collectors to fishermen, philosophers to revolutionaries, kings to shepherds and shepherds who became kings! No, what *really* makes the Bible unique is that each of these people was inspired to write the very words of God himself. God has spoken through this book to millions of people down the centuries and continues to do so today.

Unfortunately, the most treasured book on our bookshelf is too often just that - on our bookshelf. Whether it is because we are too busy, too self-reliant or too scared to hear God speak, survey results confirm that only a quarter of Christians open the Bible outside of a Sunday service. This waste of a precious resource would make William Tyndale turn in his grave. I can't help but be moved when I read about the incredible lengths that he went to to translate the Latin Bible into 'ploughboy' English. Just before they broke his neck, he managed one last cry, 'May God open the eyes of the King of England.' What the King couldn't see then is what we sometimes can't see now – the value of having God's words available to read in our own homes in our own language. That is what Tyndale, along with Wycliffe and others, suffered for: not the privilege of being able to stick God's Word on our shelves – but rather to have God's words stick in our hearts and lives.

The irony is that there are still people around the world who would do anything to be able to hold and read a Bible in their own language. There is a scene in the video for Linkin Park's song, 'What I've done', which shows an overweight man stuffing his face with an enormous greasy burger before cutting to a girl who is wasting away due to anorexia, then cutting to a malnourished famine victim starving to death. One person binges while another one starves; one starves because they won't eat while another starves because they can't eat. This image of unequally distributed resources can also be applied to the Bible. Millions of people around the world have no access to the Bible in a language that they can understand, while every day we walk past bookshops crammed full of Bibles in different translations, paraphrases, bindings and formats, which remain unused and unopened. There are people almost starving to death spiritually, through no choice of their own, while we in the West suffer from biblical anorexia.

In order to tackle our lack of appetite for the Bible, as well as the lack of Bibles for those who have the appetite, more than fifty agencies, organizations, denominations, festivals and colleges have united under the banner of Biblefresh. In 2011 it will be the 400th anniversary of the King James Version of the Bible – a translation that has shaped our culture in myriad ways – and we are praying that together this year we will rediscover the sweetness of the Bible as honey on our tongues, the challenge of the Bible as a sword that cuts to our hearts and the comfort of the Bible as the rock of truth on which we can stand. Biblefresh is an opportunity to see how God's words really can bring change in our lives, our churches, our communities and our world.

You don't have to wait until 2011 to get involved. Register your personal interest in the project at www.biblefresh.com or encourage your church to become a Biblefresh church. This involves pledging to raise the game in these four areas:

1. Bible Reading

With so few Christians opening the Bible outside of a church meeting, this track seeks to inspire Christians to read the Bible in fresh ways, individually, in groups and as whole churches, making use of developments in digital technology and creative publishing.

2. Bible Training

Our research tells us that only half of church leaders and a seventh of churchgoers are confident in their Bible knowledge. Forty per cent of Christians feel undermined in their confidence in Scripture after the recent militant atheism onslaught. Many Christians who teach the Bible, such as Sunday school teachers and house-group leaders, have received no training in interpreting and applying the Bible.[1] This track aims to equip Christians with improved Bible handling skills.

3. Bible Translation

With over 200 million people without the Scriptures in their own language and 2,393 language groups yet to have their own Bible, we are asking churches to give financial support to a translation project facilitated jointly by Bible Society and Wycliffe Bible Translators during 2011, enabling more people worldwide to access the Bible. At the same time, we hope that Biblefresh will equip Christians to translate the message of the Bible into their own culture and lives.

4. Bible Experiences

This track seeks to whet the appetite for biblical engagement by using film, music, drama and art to draw people back to reading and living the Bible.

This book is packed full of ideas to get you started. All the authors have generously given their work for free because they have a passion to see Christians re-engage with Scriptures, and hear stories of how worlds are being transformed. Any resource that encourages me – and others – to read, love and live the Bible is hugely welcome. I would like to express my thanks to everyone who has contributed to the production of this resource, and I add my prayer to theirs – that we will all have our eyes and ears opened to God's words afresh.

Krish Kandiah
on behalf of the Biblefresh Executive Committee

JOHN STOTT

THE PURPOSE OF THE BIBLE

The choice of a book to read and the way in which we read it are determined largely by the author's purpose in writing it. Is it a textbook of science or history intended to inform, or a novel meant purely to entertain? Is it a piece of serious prose or poetry in which the writer reflects on life and stimulates the reader to think about it too? Does it speak in any meaningful way to the contemporary world? Or is it perhaps a controversial work in which he deliberately sets out to argue his point of view? Moreover, is the author qualified to write on the subject? Questions like these are often in our minds when we ask, 'Is it worth reading?'

Most books supply prospective readers with the information they want about who wrote them and why. Either the author tells us candidly in a preface about himself and his object in writing, or the publisher does so in the 'blurb' on the cover. Most readers spend time examining these before committing themselves to buy, borrow or read the book.

It is a great pity that readers of the Bible do not always ask the same questions. Many appear to pick it up and begin their reading at random. Some start at Genesis and get stuck in Leviticus. Others may doggedly persevere from a sense of duty, even setting (and achieving) a target of reading the whole Bible through section by section in five years, but without deriving much benefit from their study because they lack understanding of the book's overall purpose. Or indeed many give up Bible reading altogether, or never start it, because they

cannot see how the tale of a faraway people in a faraway age could have any relevance for them today.

In any case, how can the Bible, which in fact is not a book but a library of sixty-six books, possibly be said to have a 'purpose'? Was it not compiled by different authors at different times with different objectives? Yes and no. There is indeed a wide variety of human author and theme. Yet behind these, Christians believe, there lies a single divine Author with a single unifying theme.

The Bible itself declares what this theme is. It is stated several times in several places, but perhaps nowhere more succinctly than by the apostle Paul to Timothy:

From infancy you have known the holy Scriptures, which are able to make you wise for salvation through

6

**faith in Christ Jesus. All Scripture is God-breathed and
is useful for teaching, rebuking, correcting and training
in righteousness, so that the man of God may be
thoroughly equipped for every good work.**
(2 Timothy 3:15–17, NIV)

Here the apostle brings together both the origin and the object
of Scripture, where it comes from and what it is intended for.
Its origin: 'God-breathed'. Its object: 'useful' for human beings.
Indeed, it is useful for us only because it is God-breathed –
inspired by God.

A book of salvation

Perhaps no biblical word has suffered more from misuse
and misunderstanding than the word 'salvation'. Some of us
Christians are to blame for the caricature of it which we have
presented to the world. As a result, the word 'salvation' has
become for many a source of embarrassment, even an object
of ridicule. We need to rescue it from the narrow concept to
which we have often debased it. For 'salvation' is a big and
noble word, as I shall soon elaborate. Salvation is freedom.
Yes, and renewal too; ultimately the renewal of the whole
cosmos.

Now the supreme purpose of the Bible, Paul writes
to Timothy, is to instruct its readers 'for salvation'. This
immediately indicates that Scripture has a practical purpose,
and that this purpose is moral rather than intellectual. Or
rather its intellectual instruction (its 'wisdom', as the Greek
word implies) is given with a view to the moral experience
called 'salvation'.

In order to grasp more firmly this positive purpose of
Scripture, it may be helpful to contrast it with some purposes
it does not have.

Firstly, the purpose of the Bible is not scientific. This is
not to say that the teaching of Scripture and of science are in
conflict with one another for, when we keep each to its proper
sphere and discern what each is affirming, they are not.
Indeed, if the God of truth is the author of both, they could
not be. Nor is it to say that the two spheres never overlap
and that nothing in the Bible has any scientific relevance, for
the Bible does contain statements of fact which can be (and
in many cases have been) scientifically verified. For example,
a number of historical facts are recorded, such as that
Nebuchadnezzar King of Babylon besieged, took and virtually
destroyed Jerusalem, and that Jesus of Nazareth was born
when Augustus was Emperor of Rome. What I am asserting
rather is that, though the Bible may contain some science, the
purpose of the Bible is not scientific.

Science (or at least natural science) is a body of knowledge
painstakingly acquired by observation, experiment and

**Praise be to the
Lord, the God of
Israel, because
he has come and
has redeemed his
people.**

induction. The purpose of God through Scripture, however, has been to disclose truths which could not be discovered by this method (called by scientists the 'empirical' method), but would have remained unknown and undiscovered if he had not revealed them. For instance, science may be able to tell us something about our physical origins (even this is an open question); only the Bible reveals our nature, both our unique nobility as creatures made in the Creator's image and our degradation as self-centred sinners in revolt against our Creator.

Next, the purpose of the Bible is not literary. Some years ago a book was published entitled *The Bible Designed to Be Read as Literature*. It was beautifully produced. The traditional verse arrangement was abandoned. And the layout indicated plainly what was poetry and what was prose. All this was helpful. Further, no one can deny, whatever his or her beliefs or disbeliefs, that the Bible does contain noble literature. It deals with the great themes of human life and destiny, and handles them with simplicity, insight and imagination. So fine was its original translation in some countries, such as England and Germany, that the Bible has become part of the nation's literary heritage. Nevertheless, God did not design the Bible as great literature. It contains some glaring stylistic weaknesses. The New Testament was written largely in *koiné* Greek, the everyday language of market and office, and much of it lacks literary polish, even grammatical accuracy. The purpose of the Bible is to be found in its message, not in its style.

Thirdly, the purpose of the Bible is not philosophical. Of course Scripture contains profound wisdom, in fact the wisdom of God. But some of the great themes with which philosophers have always wrestled are not given a thorough treatment in Scripture. Take the great problems of suffering and evil. As phenomena of human experience they figure prominently throughout the Bible. On almost every page men and women sin, and men and women suffer. And some light is thrown - supremely by the cross - on both problems. But no ultimate explanation of either is offered, nor are the ways of God justified in relation to them, in terms acceptable to human philosophy. Even in the Book of Job, which concentrates on the problem of suffering, Job in the end humbles himself before God without understanding God's providence. I think the reason is simply that the Bible is more a practical than a theoretical book. It is more concerned to tell us how to bear suffering and overcome evil than it is to philosophize about their origin and purpose.

So the Bible is primarily a book neither of science, nor of literature, nor of philosophy, but of salvation.

In saying this we must give the word 'salvation' its broadest possible meaning. Salvation is far more than merely the forgiveness of sins. It includes the whole sweep of God's purpose to redeem and restore humankind, and indeed all creation. What we claim for the Bible is that it unfolds God's total plan.

It begins with the creation, so that we may know the divine likeness in which we were made, the obligations which we have repudiated and the heights from which we have fallen. We can understand neither what we are in sin nor what we may be by grace until we know what we once were by creation.

The Bible goes on to tell us how sin entered into the world, and death as a result of sin. It emphasizes the gravity of sin as a revolt against the authority of God our Creator and Lord, and the justice of his judgement upon it. There are many salutary warnings in Scripture about the perils of disobedience.

But the main thrust of the biblical message is that God loves the very rebels who deserve nothing at his hand but judgement. Before time began, Scripture says, his plan of salvation took shape. It originated in his grace, his free and unmerited mercy. He made with Abraham a covenant of grace, promising through his posterity to bless all the families of the earth. The rest of the Old Testament is devoted to an account of his gracious dealings with Abraham's posterity, the people of Israel. In spite of their obstinate rejection of his Word, as it came to them through law and prophets, he never cast them off. They broke the covenant, not he.

The historical coming of Jesus Christ was in fulfilment of his covenant:

> **Praise be to the Lord, the God of Israel,**
> **because he has come and has redeemed his people.**
> **He has raised up a horn of salvation for us**
> **in the house of his servant David**
> **(as he said through his holy prophets of long ago),**
> **salvation from our enemies**
> **and from the hand of all who hate us –**
> **to show mercy to our fathers**
> **and to remember his holy covenant,**
> **the oath he swore to our father Abraham:**
> **to rescue us from the hand of our enemies,**
> **and to enable us to serve him without fear**
> **in holiness and righteousness before him all our days.**
> **(Luke 1:68–75, NIV)**

It is important to observe that the promised 'salvation' from 'our enemies' is understood in terms of 'holiness and righteousness' and - later in the same passage - of 'the forgiveness of their sins, because of the tender mercy of our God'.

So the New Testament concentrates on the outworking of this salvation, on the way of 'forgiveness' and of 'holiness' through Jesus Christ's death, resurrection and gift of the Holy

The Bible is primarily a book neither of science, nor of literature, nor of philosophy, but of salvation.

Spirit. The apostles emphasize that forgiveness is possible only through the sin-bearing death of Christ, and a new birth leading to a new life only through the Spirit of Christ. Then the letters are full of practical ethical instruction. As the New English Bible translates 2 Timothy 3:16, Scripture is profitable not only 'for teaching the truth and refuting error' but 'for reformation of manners and discipline in right living.' It also portrays Christ's church as the society of the saved, who are called to a life of sacrificial service and witness in the world.

Finally, the New Testament authors insist that although God's people have already in one sense been saved, in another their salvation lies still in the future. We are given the promise that one day our bodies will be redeemed. 'In this hope we were saved' (Romans 8:24). And in this final redemption the whole creation will somehow be involved. If we are to be clothed with new bodies, there is also going to be a new heaven and a new earth pervaded by righteousness alone. Then and only then, with no sin either in our nature or in our society, will God's salvation be complete. The glorious liberty of God's children will be the freedom to serve. God will be everything to everybody (Romans 8:21; 1 Corinthians 15:28).

Such is the comprehensive salvation set forth in Scripture. Conceived in a past eternity, achieved at a point in time and historically worked out in human experience, it will reach its consummation in the eternity of the future. The Bible is unique in its claim to instruct us for 'such a great salvation' (Hebrews 2:3).

John Stott is Rector Emeritus of All Souls Church, Langham Place and the author of fifty books.

Taken from *Understanding the Bible* by John Stott (Scripture Union, 1984). Used by Permission.

NEW
NIV BIBLES
FROM HODDER

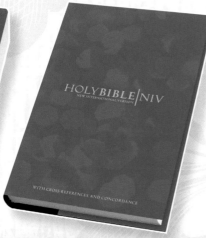

**NIV POPULAR ORANGE
PAPERBACK BIBLE**
9780340979587
£11.99

**NIV CROSS-REFERENCE BLUE
HARDBACK BIBLE**
9780340979501
£17.99

**NIV POCKET RED
NOTEBOOK BIBLE**
9780340996195
£15.99

**NIV POCKET SLATE
HARDBACK BIBLE**
9780340979662
£10.99

RICHARD FOSTER

SEEING THE BIBLE
AFRESH

I am about to do a new thing;
now it springs forth, do you not perceive it?
I will make a way in the wilderness
and rivers in the desert.

Isaiah 43:19 (NRSV)

God has given us a written revelation of who God is and of what God's purposes are for humanity. And God has chosen to accomplish this great work through the People of God on earth. This written revelation now resides as a massive fact at the heart of human history. There is, simply, no book that is remotely close to achieving the significance and influence of the Bible. It is truly The Book (*hay Biblos*).

But the intrinsic power and greatness of the Bible does not make it easy for us to receive the life it offers. The average 'Bible consumer', publishing research tells us, owns nine Bibles and is looking for more. This is mute but powerful testimony to a deep and abiding sense of *lack* - a sense that we have not really achieved a grasp of the Bible that is adequate to our needs.

In point of fact, we can often use the Bible in ways that stifle spiritual life or even destroy the soul. This happened to any number of people who walked with Jesus, heard him teach, and saw him exercise the power of the kingdom of God. For many, their very study of the Scriptures prevented them from recognizing who he was and from putting their confidence in him (John 5:39-47). And later, Peter speaks in very grim terms of how people can 'twist' Scripture 'to their own destruction' (2 Peter 3:16).

Is it possible that this still happens today? Sadly, we must admit that it does. Think of the multiplied millions of people who say, sincerely, that the Bible is *the* guide to life but who still starve to death in the presence of its spiritual feast. This tragic situation is obvious from the usual effects (or lack of effects) that the study of the Bible has in the daily lives of people, even among those who speak most highly of it.

The Source of the Problem

The source of the problem is rooted in the two most common objectives people have for studying the Bible. The first is the practice of studying the Bible for information or knowledge alone. This may include information about particular facts or historical events, or knowledge of general truths or doctrines, or even knowledge of how others are mistaken in their religious views, beliefs, and practices.

We know from experience how knowledge can make people arrogant - even knowledge of the Bible and of God. It is not surprising, then, that study that focuses on knowledge alone does not lead to life transformation, which is the real human need. No wonder we who love the Bible keep buying more editions of it, hoping to obtain what we know in our hearts is there for us.

The second common objective people often have for studying the Bible is to find some formula that will solve the pressing need of the moment. Thus we seek out lists of specific passages that speak to particular needs rather than seeking whole-life discipleship to Jesus. To be sure, these needs are important, desperately so when we are trapped in the harsh realities of life. They can involve anything from needs for comfort or forgiveness, to physical healing, to conformity to a particular denominational or political persuasion, to special endowments or gifts of the Spirit, to works of social liberation. But in the end they always have to do with being 'a good citizen', 'a good spouse', or 'a good something else' – perhaps even with being 'a good Christian' by certain interpretations.

What we must face up to about these two common objectives for studying the Bible is that they always leave us or someone else in charge. They are, in fact, ways of trying to control what comes out of the Bible rather than entering the process of the transformation of our whole person and of our whole life into *Christlikeness.*

If we want to receive from the Bible the life 'with God' that is portrayed in the Bible, we must be prepared to have our dearest and most fundamental assumptions about ourselves and our associations called into question. We must read humbly and in a constant attitude of repentance. Only in this way can we gain a thorough and practical grasp of the spiritual riches that God has made available to all humanity in his written Word. Only in this way can we keep from transforming The Book into a Catholic Bible, an Orthodox Bible, a Protestant Bible, an 'Ours Is More Accurate than Yours' Bible.

What will enable us to avoid this soul-crushing result?

The Supernatural Power of Love

Jesus founded on earth a new type of community, and in it and through him, love – God-given *agape* love – came down to live with power on earth. Now, it is this God-given *agape* love that transforms our lives and gives us true spiritual substance as persons. Suppose, then, we simply agreed that the proper outcome of studying the Bible is growth in the supernatural power of love: love of God and of all people?

We could call this The First Corinthians 13 Test: 'If I . . . understand all mysteries and all knowledge, and if I have all faith, so as to remove mountains, but do not have love, I am nothing' (verse 2, NASB). And so the test of whether or not we have really gotten the point of the Bible would then be the quality of love that we show.

Knowledge of the Bible and its teachings would, of course, continue to be of great value, but only insofar as it leads to greater love: to greater appropriation of God's love for us and for us to have greater love for God, others, and ourselves. When we turn to Scripture in this way, our reason for 'knowing' the Bible and everything it teaches would be that we might love more and know more of love. We would experience this love not as an abstraction but as a practical reality by which we are possessed. And since all those who love through and through obey the law, we would become ever more obedient to Jesus Christ and his Abba Father.

Regarding the Bible, then, perhaps the most basic question is: Shall we try to control the Bible, that is, try to make it 'come out right,' or shall we simply seek to release its life into our lives and into our world? Shall we try to 'tilt' it this way or that, or shall we give it complete freedom to 'tilt' us as it will?

Can we surrender freely to the life we see in the Bible, or must we remain in control of that life, only selectively endorsing it so far as we find it proper and safe from our 'perspective'? Can we trust the living water that flows from Christ through the Bible, open ourselves to it and open it up into the world as best we can, and then get out of its way? This is the goal of reading the Bible for spiritual transformation.

Richard Foster is the founder of Renovaré and author of numerous books, including *Celebration of Discipline.*

Taken from *Life With God* by Richard Foster (Hodder & Stoughton, 2009). Used by Permission.

Jesus founded on earth a new type of community, and in it and through him, love.

Rob Bell

The Bible is a dangerous book. It is provocative, compelling and mysterious.

What first gave you an appetite for studying the Bible?

I began to be fascinated when I started to study Jesus as a Jewish Rabbi and began to discover that there was a Jewish conversation that Jesus was engaging with. There are great debates when Jesus was asked a question, often around a heated point of controversy in his culture. Often he is siding with either one or another of the popular positions of his day – either siding with progressives or the conservatives. The more I understood about his culture the more real he became, as opposed to kind of a lofty person detached from this world.

How can we help the church re-engage with the Bible?

The Bible is a dangerous book. It is provocative, compelling and mysterious. One of the first things is to understand that the Bible is poetry, it's historical narrative, it's gospel, it's letters. One philosopher said that familiarity breeds unfamiliarity. What happens is that people become so familiar with the Bible that it becomes unfamiliar. One of the first things is revealing to people just how much they don't know. There is a sort of humility that comes from that, which is quite intoxicating, like 'Wow I never knew that – what else did I miss?'

What is your hope for the Biblefresh initiative?

My experience has been that any time people begin to engage with the Scriptures in new and fresh ways, unbelievable things begin to happen. Written over 1,400 to 1,600 years, more than forty authors, giving their

It's sometimes strange and sometimes beautiful; sometimes quirky and sometimes hard to understand...

poems, insights, letters, stories, their memories of their encounters with God – with their understanding that history is headed somewhere, that we are not alone and abandoned, and God is not detached, but there's a story that is unfolding in the midst of human history. It's sometimes odd, it's sometimes strange and sometimes beautiful; sometimes quirky and sometimes hard to understand; sometimes it grabs you by the shoulders and shakes you. When people begin to get in touch with this book and this story and begin to embrace it – all of its easy to access truth and all of the hard things and the questions that it raises – when people begin to get in touch with this and embrace it and jump into it, then all sorts of things happen. So the Biblefresh initiative – who knows what it will lead to, but it will be interesting and unforgettable.

Rob Bell is a writer and speaker and founding pastor of Mars Hill Bible Church in Michigan. He is author of *Velvet Elvis* (new ed. Zondervan, 2006).

© Mike North 2009

ROB COTTON

THE BIBLEFRESH YEAR: WHAT COULD 2011 LOOK LIKE FOR MY CHURCH?

You're a busy church leader with 101 demands upon you each and every day. So how can you begin to think about taking on one more thing? Biblefresh will offer many opportunities to engage with the Bible in new ways, but is flexible enough for you to shape it to fit the needs of your church and your community.

To help you get started, on the following pages is a structure for 2011, which suggests how you might include a focal point for each of the four streams. Many churches found it really helpful during Hope 08 to have a few 'hooks' or high points upon which they could develop their own activity and response to the local situation. So these are just a few ideas to spark your own creativity and give you permission to dream up something that would work for your context.

Many churches will attempt projects which they have never done before and which will hopefully continue long into the future as part of the legacy of Biblefresh. The challenge to move people forward in their relationship with the Bible should not be underestimated, but if churches are prepared to accept it, the experience will transform our churches and people's lives.

Preparing for Biblefresh – The Coming

It is important that churches prepare their members if they are to participate fully in Biblefresh and get the most out of this opportunity. The season of Advent has traditionally been a period to prepare spiritually for the coming of Christ at Christmas, but it can also be an important time of focused prayer, building expectancy in people's hearts and minds, as we enter the year of Biblefresh.

Even if you wouldn't usually do so, you might want to pray the BCP's Collect for the Second Sunday in Advent, which is focused on the Bible:

> Blessed Lord,
> Who caused all holy Scriptures to be written for our learning:
> Help us so to hear them,
> Read, mark, learn and inwardly digest them,
> That through patience and the comfort of your holy word
> We may embrace and ever hold fast
> The hope of everlasting life,
> Which you have given us
> In our Saviour Jesus Christ.

You might want to do something fresh and different during the Advent season to profile Biblefresh and the idea of engaging the Bible in new ways. For example, BRF have developed something called Paperless Christmas (www. paperlesschristmas.org.uk). Short video clips entitled *The Adventures of Mary and Joseph – The Road Movie* can be used in worship, schools or family events. BRF have also produced a set of creative activities to be used in conjunction with each of the nine videos. These will enable children and adults to work with the Christmas story in a thoughtful and fun way: www.barnabasinschools.org.uk/paperlesschristmas

Launching Biblefresh – Covenant

The way a campaign begins can influence the level of commitment from churches and their members. Why not launch Biblefresh with a special church service? You could invite people in the congregation to share testimonies about how their lives have been shaped by the Bible, as well as praying for the initiative and sharing plans for the year ahead.

Why not take the commitment a step further and covenant together to engage with Scripture in fresh ways? Unlike New Year's resolutions, which are usually broken within days or weeks, if you make a pledge together as a church, you could start something which could become a way of life. You might want to use the Methodist Covenant Prayer as you make your commitment:

I am no longer my own but yours.
Put me to what you will,
Rank me with whom you will;
Put me to doing,
Put me to suffering;
Let me be employed for you
Or laid aside for you,
Exalted for you
Or brought low for you;
Let me be full,
Let me be empty,
Let me have all things,
Let me have nothing;
I freely and wholeheartedly yield all things
To your pleasure and disposal.
And now,
Glorious and blessed God,
Father, Son and Holy Spirit,
You are mine and I am yours.
So be it.
And the covenant now made on earth,
Let it be ratified in heaven. Amen.

Other ideas:

- Covenant as a church to do something new in each stream – reading, training, translation and experience. For example, you could agree as a church to read through the Bible in a year; attend a festival together for some training; donate your charitable giving to Bible translation; host an experience, such as a *Miracles of Jesus* DVD discussion group (www.miraclesofjesus. co.uk). Check the 'Freshen Up' sections of this book and the Biblefresh website for ideas and resources (www.biblefresh.com).

- Hold a Bible overview experience, one evening or weekend, to give people the big picture right from the start. There are lots of resources to help you, such as *The Word in One* (Nationwide Christian Trust).

- Hold an area-wide Biblefresh launch, for example, during the Week of Prayer for Christian Unity or another joint service.

Easter – The Cross

This is a great opportunity to host a Bible experience, within the church or out in the local community. Some ideas to get you thinking are:

- Hold a public Bible reading marathon, inviting local dignitaries and key community figures to read the Passion passages.

- Galvanize local churches to take part in a Good Friday procession, carrying the cross from a church to a public space, followed by a silent vigil or a public reading of the crucifixion narratives.

- Perform one of the Mystery Plays based upon the Easter story, involving people from a number of local churches. Winchester Churches Together recently did this and also involved local businesses and community groups.

- Show the film *The Passion of the Christ* or another Easter-themed film and host a discussion group afterwards. Or borrow an idea from a group of churches in Coventry, who recently hosted a viewing of the critically acclaimed *Son of Man* film at the Warwick Arts Centre, which tells the story of Jesus through a tale of corruption and redemption in modern-day Africa.

CASE STUDY: THE BIGGER PICTURE, LOUGHBOROUGH, LEICESTERSHIRE

The Bigger Picture was an innovative, world record-breaking attempt staged in Loughborough over the Easter period. This Loughborough Churches Partnership project involved 19 church congregations, coming together to paint the biggest paint-by-numbers community picture in the world.

The painting was comprised of over 500 ply-board paint panels, totalling 80 metres in length and standing 8.6 metres from the ground to the highest point – the length of a football pitch and the height of a house. They used about 236 litres of paint and each panel was painted by various community groups, schools, churches, families and individuals, overseen by a local artist.

The painting depicted the events of Passion Week: Jesus' entry into Jerusalem; the cleansing of the Temple; the last supper; Gethsemane; the trial of Jesus; the crucifixion; the burial; the resurrection and Jesus on the Emmaus road.

The Bigger Picture reached its peak on Easter Monday with a fun day, barbecue, concert and firework display attended by approximately 1,300 people. It also included a ceremony for putting the last piece of the picture in place, making a new world record.

The concept came from Revd Phil Weaver, one of the ministers in the town: 'Many people know just snippets of the Bible story but aren't that familiar with the full story and real meaning of Easter. The Bigger Picture was an ideal opportunity not only to engage the community but also to enable us to retell the life-transforming story of Easter in a creative way.'

In total approximately 2,000 people from within the community took part in creating the artwork and many more came to view and photograph this extraordinary piece of art. Each person received a souvenir brochure outlining the full Easter story. The Bigger Picture certainly created a community buzz and captured the imagination of the whole town.

Pentecost – Communication

When the Holy Spirit filled the disciples, people from many different backgrounds and cultures heard them speaking in their own language, understood their words and became followers of Jesus. The church's challenge today continues to be communicating the message of Jesus in every language and in culturally appropriate ways.

But for many, the need is still simply for access to a Bible that they can understand. Over 200 million people do not have the Scriptures in their own language and 2,393 language groups are without a Bible. The story of Pentecost is a great way to focus the church's attention on this need and encourage giving towards the Biblefresh translation project in Burkina Faso. There are dozens of resources to help highlight the issues around Bible availability, which can be used in church services.

For more ideas on the wider themes of Bible Translation, go to the 'Freshen Up' article at the end of the Translation section.

Harvest – Cultivation

In the autumn months, harvest festival is the high point in the church calendar, providing a means to draw alongside fringe members of the church and the local community, particularly in rural areas. The biblical imagery of God as a sower and his Word as a seed helps us to make direct links to the Bible in ways that are simple and understandable. So this autumn, why not . . .

- 'Bed in' the learning that took place during the summer festivals, by establishing Bible discussion groups and encourage ongoing grappling with the Scriptures.

- At the start of the academic year, you could take up an opportunity for some training at your nearest Bible college or through an online provider. Many colleges will be running special courses for those who are lay leaders, some of which will be during evenings or weekends – as well as refresher courses for church leaders. (See the Bible Training map for more suggestions.)

- Theme a service around the parables relating to sowing and reaping and use the time to remind people about the covenant at the start of the year. You could plant mustard seeds as a creative act of worship and re-commit to growing God's Word in our lives.

- Profile Scripture engagement on Bible Sunday and make use of the resources on the website (www.biblesunday.org).

- Consider hosting a flower festival around favourite Bible passages, stories and themes.
- As the nights draw in, you could get cosy in a café or pub and start up a Lyfe group (www.lyfe.org.uk).

Christmas – Celebration

Churches receive more visitors during the Christmas celebrations than at any other, so it's a wonderful opportunity to engage people creatively with the Scriptures. Many churches experiment with alternative acts of worship, or invite people to visit the crib or the stable. Some church members re-enact the key scenes of the Christmas story – complete with the obligatory tea towel as a shepherd.

The Baptist Union run a great initiative where local churches set up a nativity scene in the town centre and invite passers-by to have their picture taken in biblical costumes. The pictures are then made available for people to download from the website www.getinthepicture.org.uk – which also helps people to understand the Bible stories that make up the Christmas story.

As you celebrate the birth of Christ, together as a church you can pause, look back and give thanks for a year of enrichment through rediscovering the life-changing power of God's Word.

Rob Cotton is the Biblefresh Network Co-ordinator. You can contact him for further advice at rob.cotton@biblesociety.org.uk or r.cotton@eauk.org

As you celebrate the birth of Christ, together as a church you can pause, look back and give thanks for a year of enrichment.

CELEBRATE

Now I can taste the difference

OPENING IT UP

BIBLE READING

NAOMI STARKEY

A GUILTY SECRET

According to a recent Bible Society survey,[1] more than 90 per cent of church leaders believe that the Bible provides 'the basic framework for our relationship with God' and 'shows us who God is, what he has done and what he is like' – yet less than half (47 per cent) feel 'very confident' in their knowledge of the Bible. Just over half of non-leaders (57 per cent) believe that the Bible should shape their daily life 'a great deal' – but just 14 per cent say that they feel 'very confident' in their Bible knowledge.

While both leaders and non-leaders are aware that knowing and using Scripture is an important part of Christian discipleship, it is surprising to find that only 58 per cent of leaders read the Bible daily, while no more than 35 per cent of non-leaders do so. The statistics add up to a picture that offers encouragement (people certainly know that the Bible matters) but also food for thought (they don't know it as well as perhaps they could).

'Not reading my Bible enough' is up there with 'not praying enough' and 'not being a good enough Christian' as ways in which believers beat themselves up spiritually and emotionally. I've lost count of the number of 'mighty men of God' I've heard about, who apparently managed three hours of Bible study and intercession before breakfast, every day. Maybe some people are inspired by hearing such stories; many more will simply feel discouraged and decide to give up altogether. The gap between ideal and reality is just too great.

If we know that the Bible is important, why do we struggle to read it? Why does it seem like a luxury rather than a necessity, when it comes to how we apportion our time? After all, we have the biggest choice of translations ever, a vast array of helpful resources available – from daily reading notes to websites – and we are free to read it pretty much wherever and whenever we please, unlike believers in some parts of the world today.

Even if we have been Christians for years, even if we feel we know the Bible inside out and word for word, we can still fail to connect it with how we live here and now. By contrast, when people first come to faith, they often find they cannot get enough of Scripture. They may have known it before, but now the stories and teaching spring into new life, because they have connected with the One who inspired it.

Perhaps we should be alert to the fact that feeling less than inspired about the Word of God indicates that we need to focus on deepening our relationship with him, never underestimating how much he longs to speak to us. However empty and dry our faith may feel, if we start to seek God's presence, he will come, gently but surely, to embrace us through his Holy Spirit and surround us with his love.

Then, through the work of the living Word, God's Word will come alive for us. Then – who knows? – we may find we actually want to emulate those mighty men of God (although perhaps not for *three* hours a day, at least not to start with). Then we may find we can truthfully say with the psalmist, 'your word is a lamp to my feet and a light for my path' (Psalm 119:105, NIV), and we cannot think of continuing our journey without it.

IF WE KNOW THAT THE BIBLE IS IMPORTANT, WHY DO WE STRUGGLE TO READ IT?

Naomi Starkey is Commissioning Editor for BRF's adult list and also edits *New Daylight* Bible reading notes.

IT CHANGED MY WORLD:

'The last two years have been the darkest of my fifty years on this planet, with the break-up of my marriage and separation from my three children. But I have found that God in his wonderful mercy, love and grace has kept my head above water and then moved me on into a greater knowledge of him and his ways. He is a great Father and a wonderful Lord and there can be no better way of experiencing his love than through the fires of suffering.

A major support through this period has been the discipline of studying God's Word. I have come to fully appreciate that being immersed and absorbed into God's Word is essential for all followers of Christ. Just as we need food and water to grow and sustain physical life, so we should hungrily feed on God's Word to grow our relationship with God and know where he is leading our lives.' **Kevin**

These true stories, used throughout the book, have been provided by people who have been using an inductive study method produced by Precept Ministries

CHANGE

Over **10** Million people can now be impacted by the Bible through UCB Christian Radio

2.5 Million people have been impacted by the Word of God last year through UCB's free resources

UCB offers free daily devotionals, *The Word For Today* and the youth version, the *Word 4U 2Day* along with *The Book of Hope*; the Gospel aimed at children.

If you or your church would like to receive these resources call 0845 60 40 401 or visit ucb.co.uk

ANTONY BILLINGTON

FIVE
REASONS NOT TO READ THE BIBLE

Some of us struggle with the Bible because we have questions about how it was put together, or we wonder about its trustworthiness, or we are troubled by its apparent sexism and violence in places. Important issues like these are addressed elsewhere in this book, and more fully by Amy Orr-Ewing in *Why Trust the Bible?* (IVP, 2008). But many of us struggle to read the Bible in the first place for more mundane – though no less real – reasons.

1. It's too long

It has 780,000 words (or thereabouts) which is quite long. But only what we might expect from an account which moves from the beginning of all things to the restoration of all things. Only what we might expect from a book which – although it tells one story - is itself a collection of different types of literature, like a library. Those of us who are daunted by its sheer length – or find reading difficult – should not feel guilty for breaking it down into doable chunks, perhaps starting out with some of the shorter prophetic books or letters, or reflecting on some of the Psalms, or working through one of the gospels.

2. It's too difficult

In part, yes. Like any learning experience – in education or at work – there will be moments of challenge in reading the Bible which make the delight of discovery that much sweeter. And it reminds us of the need to draw on the wisdom and expertise of others to help us along the way. But in many respects, much of the Bible is relatively straightforward. We *can* understand it, even as we recognize the ongoing need to explore it more fully and work through its significance for our relationship with God and each other.

3. It's too boring

Although we may find some parts of the Bible overly repetitive or detailed, knowing the author – God himself – can make all the difference to how we read. Moreover, as it happens, what might be dull to us is riveting to someone else. For Christians in some parts of the world, Leviticus speaks powerfully – because its emphasis on holy objects, special days and sacred places connects with cultural concerns. In other contexts, wisdom literature is crucial because it is seen as extending and completing the search for wisdom in other ancient systems of thought.

4. I'm too busy

In today's multi-tasking, multi-distracting world some people find it difficult even to find time to read the Bible. Even so, in all the busyness of life, most of us still make time for things that *really* matter to us. In fact, those who are genuinely busy, who need to live by the diary, may benefit from making it part of their schedule, getting into a routine and sticking with it.

5. I'm too tired

You're not alone. This is a common complaint, not just when it comes to reading the Bible. The competing demands of work, home, children and relationships, combined with poor eating habits and lack of fitness increase our risk of stress, depression and other health problems. Here is where careful eating and drinking habits and regular, low-level exercise might not only boost our energy levels and help with ongoing fatigue, but might also open up more moments in the day or week to spend profitable time with the Bible, settling into a regular practice that fits with the natural rhythms of life.

And so the reasons for *not* reading the Bible might stack up. Which is why we might find it helpful to reframe the issue by thinking of the reasons *for* reading the Bible. Not because it's fashionable or meets our felt needs, nor because it's a 'how to' manual or a source of golden nuggets for life, but because it is the Word of God through which he speaks to us – teaching us, challenging us, encouraging us, and shaping us in the process.

Not more than a few verses into Psalm 119 is a direct address to God by the poet, maintained to the end, where the dynamic is one of relationship, where God's Word provides the medium for the bond between the Lord and his servant, an engagement which is not about squeezing out of the Bible what's seen as directly applicable to me, but being present to a person, a loved-one no less, by attending to their words. Engaging with God's Word involves thinking, feeling, willing and doing – where minds are informed, hearts are touched, and lives are changed.

Antony Billington is Head of Faculty at the London Institute for Contemporary Christianity

licc
The London Institute for Contemporary Christianity

IT CHANGED MY WORLD:

'As I've grown in the knowledge of his Word, it has helped me to understand God better in my teen years. I simply haven't had the same doubts I've seen in my friends and I've been able to provide them with encouragements and biblical truth when they find themselves feeling unsure of God.' **Elizabeth**

KNOWLEDGE

PETER WILLIAMS

CAN WE TRUST THE BIBLE?

We all sometimes trust someone else's word.
Why do we do it?
Not usually because we have some scientific proof that what they say is correct, but most of us have pretty developed senses of whom to trust and whom not to trust.

We're generally pretty suspicious of salesmen even though they present themselves as trustworthy. We know that they tend to play up the benefits of a product and downplay its drawbacks. I remember, however, when I was looking to buy a house, being guided round an empty property by a part-time employee of an estate agent, who kept telling me all the disadvantages of the property and none of the advantages. Although I didn't buy that property, I came away with a strong impression that I had been speaking to someone whose word I could trust. I also thought that if I had been an estate agent I would not have employed him to sell properties!

In a lot of ways, the Bible is like that property guide. The writers are doing anything but trying to sell you something.

For a start, it is not written by a company of people who are out to persuade you that they are without fault. Almost without exception every major figure and group in the Bible is recorded as having had faults. The Bible was not royal propaganda written to show the great achievements of kings, nor nationalist propaganda showing the virtue of the Israelites. In the New Testament all the gospels speak of how those who became the leaders in the early church abandoned their own leader at the hour of his greatest need. So the Bible is not written by people trying to give you special confidence in themselves.

Nor are they just trying to highlight all the advantages of their product. The biblical writers are, of course, unashamed to tell us of the excellence of a God who saves, and of his plan of salvation, but even then they don't exactly give us a 'hard sell'. Throughout the Bible we are told of how difficult it is for those who truly want to follow God. So while the Bible writers obviously think that there's nothing better than being in the presence of our God, they don't generally write at length about the pleasures in heaven. The New Testament writers obviously think that there's no one greater than Jesus Christ, but even then they don't exactly engage in sale tactics. One of the striking things about the miracle reports in the Gospels is their complete lack of sensationalism. In Mark's Gospel, Jesus even tells people not to tell others about his miracles. And in the Gospels, while Jesus is constantly being said to fulfil prophecy, often in remarkable ways, it is hardly reported in a sensational manner as if some clairvoyant were advertising their credentials to tell us the future. Rather it is used to teach us about the person and mission of Jesus. Meanwhile, Jesus himself is regularly portrayed as saying things that simply don't fit with what any particular group would be inclined to believe.

It is sometimes said that Christianity is an emotional crutch, or that Christian beliefs result from wishful thinking, but Jesus is not the sort of person who would be invented or embellished to fit beliefs people wanted to have. By all accounts many of the first people to believe in Jesus were Jews, and yet Jews were hardly predisposed to believe that their great God might become a mere man. Soon after both Jews and gentiles accepted that Jesus was risen from the dead, though Jews were not naturally inclined to believe that one person might rise *before* others, and non-Jews in the Roman empire would generally have preferred a saviour to escape the physical realm after death rather than return to it through resurrection. Above all, it is hard to see what would have persuaded so many people, Jews and gentiles, to believe that someone who had been crucified – who had been publicly shown to be a loser by the Romans – could actually be the creator of the universe, who should be worshipped as Lord.

What inclined so many people to believe the Christian message, was not that it fitted with what they wanted to believe nor that it flattered them. The best explanation continues to be that Jesus genuinely ministered, died and rose again as the Gospels say, and that the resurrection transformed the disciples into bold witnesses to a message that was not at all to their own advantage. Their message involved honesty about the human position and the most compelling story of the only valid solution to the problem of human sin: that God himself should become human and die the death that we deserve. The complete absence of spin or salesmanship should be obvious to any with ears to hear.

But while the message of the gospels did not fit with what people may have wanted to hear, the descriptions in the gospels fit amazingly well with what we know of the setting of the events. Just as even a salesman may gain our respect by showing genuine knowledge not only of his product, but also of other products and of our own needs, so the gospel writers should gain our trust for the amazingly detailed knowledge they have of the time and setting of the events. They know details ranging from the architecture of the Temple, to the contours of the land, the names of small villages, the various religious groups and even personal names used. Just in passing they can let you know facts that we can now verify – whether there were cockerels in Jerusalem or a sycamore tree inside Jericho.

When you realize the depth of knowledge that they show, you soon realize that it would have been impossible for anyone to write what they wrote without either spending time where the events are supposed to have taken place or at least talking at length to people who had. These details could not be right if a significant number of the accounts resulted from garbled reports. Rather, the reports show just how much attention was given to detail. And if they were careful in the small matters, isn't there every reason to think they would have been even more careful about the larger matters?

Peter Williams is Warden of Tyndale House, Cambridge and Honorary Senior Lecturer in Biblical Studies at the University of Aberdeen.

TYNDALE HOUSE
RESIDENTIAL CENTRE FOR BIBLICAL RESEARCH

MY FAVOURITE BIBLE VERSE

ROWAN WILLIAMS
ARCHBISHOP OF CANTERBURY

'All of us have had that veil removed so that we can be mirrors that brightly reflect the glory of the Lord. And as the Spirit of the Lord works within us, we become more and more like him and reflect his glory even more.' (2 Corinthians 3:18)

This verse tells us that what God reveals in Jesus is nothing less than his full, true nature; and that we, if we let his Spirit work in us, come to reflect that. It is the most daring promise in the Bible!

Reproduced with permission from Words for Life *by Wycliffe Bible Translators*

PETER S. WILLIAMS

AN ATHEIST'S GUIDE TO THE GOSPELS

Consider the sort of thing atheist Richard Dawkins says about the gospels: 'Ever since the nineteenth century, scholarly theologians have made an overwhelming case that the gospels are not reliable accounts of what happened . . . All were written long after the death of Jesus . . . then copied and recopied, through many different "Chinese Whispers generations" . . . Nobody knows who the four evangelists were, but they almost certainly never met Jesus . . . Much of what they wrote was in no sense an honest attempt at history . . . It is even possible to mount a serious, though not widely supported, historical case that Jesus never lived at all . . . reputable Bible scholars do not in general regard the New Testament . . . as a reliable record of what actually happened in history.' [1]

First, we must see through Dawkins's rhetorical ploy of implying that anyone who thinks the gospels are reliable 'accounts of what happened' are by definition unscholarly people whose *disreputable* opinions are *out of date*. Indeed, if anyone's New Testament scholarship is out of date, it's Dawkins's!

Second, we must distinguish *philosophical* doubts about revelation from evidential questions about history. Dawkins is swayed by David Hume's notorious scepticism about miracles, but as William Lane Craig writes: 'those who are familiar with contemporary philosophy . . . know that Hume's arguments are today widely rejected as fallacious.' [2] If one is even *agnostic* about the existence of God, then one must be open to the possibility of miraculous revelation, for as Antony Flew affirms: 'You cannot limit the possibilities of omnipotence except to produce the logically impossible. Everything else is open to omnipotence.' [3]

Third, we must consider the historical evidence. Craig L. Blomberg observes that, by combining evidence from first- to third-century Greco-Roman writers, 'one can clearly accumulate enough evidence to refute the fanciful notion that Jesus never existed . . . [This evidence includes] references to his crucifixion, being worshipped as a god, working miracles, having an unusual birth, and being viewed as a sage, king and an instigator of a controversy . . .' [4]

There's good evidence that the gospels we have today closely resemble the original editions. Flew acknowledges that 'the textual authority, the earliness and the number of manuscripts for most of the Christian documents, is unusually great . . . that's . . . very good authority for the accuracy of the text . . .' [5] According to Winfried Corduan: 'No other ancient document equals the New Testament when it comes to the preservation of manuscripts, both in terms of number and closeness in time to the original autographs.'[6]

Scholars agree that all four gospels were written within c. 60 years of Jesus' death, starting with Mark within c. 40 years of Jesus' death. As Carsten Peter Thiede comments: 'those who argue for early dates of authentic Gospels as sources of information about an historical Jesus . . . are no longer the conservative or fundamentalist outsiders.'[7]

J.P. Moreland affirms that 'a strong case could be made for the fact that much of the New Testament, including the Gospels and the sources behind them, was written by eyewitnesses.'[8] Christians probably wouldn't attribute gospels to peripheral characters like Mark, Luke, and even Matthew, unless they really wrote them. Indeed, 'according to the best evidence available from the early years of the church, three of the four gospels are directly linked to the apostles; the fourth, Luke, by his own testimony (Luke 1:1-4), was dependent on eyewitnesses and those who had known Jesus from the beginning.'[9] Many of the eyewitnesses were martyred for the claims they made about Jesus, a fact that at least speaks to their honesty.

The New Testament letters 'date mainly from the period AD 49-69, and provide confirmation of the importance and interpretations of Jesus in this formative period.'[10] In particular, 'a concept of a divine Jesus was already present, at the latest, within sixteen to twenty years after the crucifixion.'[11] Paul's letters contain creeds and hymns (e.g. Romans 1:3-4; 1 Corinthians 11:23 ff.; 15:3-8; Philippians 2:6-11; Colossians 1:15-18; 1 Timothy 2:8) that had become 'standard, recognized creeds and hymns well before their incorporation into Paul's letters.'[12] These sources, from the first decades of Christianity: 'consistently present a portrait of a miraculous and divine Jesus who rose from the dead . . .'[13] Belief in the divinity of Jesus stems 'from the first, eyewitness generation.'[14]

Hence we may agree with Blomberg that: 'The gospels may be accepted as trustworthy accounts of what Jesus did and said . . . other conclusions, widespread though they are, seem not to stem from even-handed historical analysis but from religious or philosophical prejudice.'[15]

THE GOSPELS MAY BE ACCEPTED AS TRUSTWORTHY ACCOUNTS OF WHAT JESUS DID AND SAID

Peter S. Williams works for the Damaris Trust and is author of *A Sceptic's Guide to Atheism* (Paternoster, 2009).

IT CHANGED MY WORLD:

'Whilst studying the Bible, God held me and kept me when things were falling to pieces.' **Jill**

HELD

AMY ORR-EWING

WHAT ABOUT THE CANON?

Let us begin by defining our terms. The word 'canon' comes from the Greek word *kanon*, meaning 'reed'. The reed was used as a measuring rod and has connotations of a standard or a fixed measuring point. The word 'canon' applied to Scripture means 'a limited and defined group of writings which are accepted as authoritative within the Christian Church'.[1] But did a group of men just randomly decide which books were in and which were out?

The New Testament canon

The churches preserved the writings of the apostles and the Gospels from the very time of the apostles' presence in their midst, whilst the letters and books were being written. The fact that these were then so widely made known and multiplied meant that one part of the church could act as a check and balance with another, making forgeries unlikely. The communion of the different parts of the church with each other meant that mistakes and frauds could be guarded against.

The manuscript tradition of the New Testament is preserved in great numbers from different places around the globe. We have distinct streams of manuscripts which come to us now from the time of the events they record and preserved in different languages – the same text of the New Testament with minor differences in spellings and occasionally different words. This wealth of manuscript material constitutes independent witnesses for the same text, existing in different parts of the world. The books which are preserved in this way are the canonical books of the New Testament. There are versions in Latin, Greek, Syriac, Coptic, Sahidic, Arabic, Ethiopic, Armenian and many other languages.

So the books of the New Testament were widely known throughout the world church and different sections were read out in church services each week.

The recognition of the books of the New Testament as scriptural was overwhelmingly a natural process, not a matter of ecclesiastical regulation. The core of the New Testament was accepted so early that subsequent rulings do no more than recognize the obvious.[2]

Where there were question marks, these were dealt with openly. With the letter of James there were questions about authorship and yet there was strong reason to believe that the writer was James the son of Zebedee or James, the brother of Jesus – both were apostles in the New Testament church. In further support of the letter of James is the fact of its inclusion in the Syriac version, as the church of Syria bordered on Palestine, where James the brother of Jesus was a bishop. Eusebius tells us that this epistle was widely received by the great majority of Christians. With the epistle to the Hebrews, questions were raised as to its authorship, but again, it was in the Syriac canon and was mentioned by many of the church Fathers and councils, and was finally included in the canon.

On the whole the New Testament books made their way into the church naturally and were accepted from the time they were written by the apostles and evangelists in the church across the world. Those books that were questioned did not come to final acceptance or rejection because of a fiat by a group of powerful men – rather, a consensus emerged in the church either recognizing authority or rejecting it.

When thinking or talking about the canon, the important concept to remember is that the church did not choose the canon; rather it officially recognized the inspiration of certain books. The inspiration of the twenty-seven books of the New Testament was already generally accepted in the early church, and when a council of church leaders met in AD 393 in Hippo and then again in 397 in Carthage, it was to confirm this and to counteract early heresies and persecution. As F.F. Bruce writes:

> When at last a Church Council – the Synod of Hippo in AD 393 – listed the twenty-seven books of the New Testament it did not confer upon them any authority which they did not already possess, but simply recorded their previously established canonicity.[3]

One of the reasons for this meeting of a church council was the increasing challenge of heresies spreading with the growing distance in time from the period when the New Testament was written. The most serious heretical challenge came from Marcion, who lived around AD 140. He distinguished between an inferior creator God of the Old Testament and God the Father revealed in Christ. He argued that the church should jettison all that pointed to the former. He wanted to expunge anything hinging at Judaism in the Bible. When this and other heretical teachings began to pose serious challenges, it became important for the church to have explicit parameters within which to work.

Amy Orr-Ewing is Training Director of RZIM Zacharias Trust and Director of Programmes for the Oxford Centre for Christian Apologetics.

Taken from *Why Trust the Bible* by Amy Orr-Ewing (IVP, 2008). Used by permission.

IT CHANGED MY WORLD:

'There is such a fantastic freedom in God's Word. We don't need gimmicks or programmes, we need his Word.' **Sally**

FREEDOM

Andy Croft

I will tell you what is written in the book of truth.

Tell us about a time when God spoke to you vividly and personally through the Bible.

I was in the middle of writing a book with a friend and had nicknamed it on my laptop for a joke 'The Book of Truth'. Having only written a couple of chapters I suddenly had a crisis of confidence – I didn't know a lot about the Bible, so why was I trying to write a book about it? In the middle of the serious questioning and doubt about the whole project I opened the Bible at random (not a prophetic technique that I had ever found very helpful but one I can't help but have a crack at every now and then!). The verse in front of me was Daniel 10:21 'but first I will tell you what is written in the Book of Truth' (NIV). Obviously I took the verse totally out of context and did all the things Bible commentators tell you not to do, but at that moment I was OK with that, I was just a bit stunned. As far as I can tell there's no other place that phrase 'Book of Truth' occurs in the Bible and certainly not with the words 'I'll tell you what's written' in it. I've since decided, having written my book, it was God's way of saying that he was going to explain to me what was written in his book, *Book of Truth*' (NIV). Maybe not the best Bible-reading technique but certainly a massive encouragement at the time!

In recent years what has helped to keep the Bible fresh for you?

Reading the Bible isn't about gathering information, how many chapters or books we've read or whether we can reel off verses from memory. It's about a relationship. Understanding this is at the heart of what it is to read the Bible and receive life from its pages. Jesus said to the Pharisees, 'You diligently study the Scriptures because you think that by them you possess eternal life. These are the Scriptures that testify about me' (John 5:39). If we read the Bible just for the sake of it, it's likely to become dry and lifeless. But if we read the Bible because we want

relationship with the Prince of Peace and the Lord of Life, then it's quite different. It becomes a way of getting to know our Friend.

The most helpful thing I've realized is that *reading the Bible keeps us fresh*: it's the water for our soul, the food for our stomach, the air for our lungs, the beat for our heart, the sugar for our tea and even the ketchup for our burger. Keeping the Bible 'fresh' isn't something that happens by putting it on an iPod or redoing the front cover. The Bible can't help but be refreshing when it leads us into the presence of God.

What does your regular practice of Bible reading look like?

For a long time I got discouraged because I'd read a bit in the morning and by lunchtime I'd have forgotten what I'd read. I suspect I may not be the only Christian who has had that experience . . . What's the point of reading the Bible if you can't remember it? A friend answered that question for me when they pointed out that when I was seven years old I ate a lot of food. I can't remember what it was, but it did me good at the time. Often we can 'pooh-pooh' the small revelations we have when we read the Bible. 'What did you learn from the Bible this week, Andy?' 'Oh not much at all, I just learnt that Jesus is compassionate, not a lot, just that.' I've discovered that reading the Bible is all about the small revelations. It's about a gentle drip drip drip. It does us good even if we can't always remember what we read.

I've found it's not always about spending hours in the Bible but reading it regularly. I tend to read the Bible in one of three ways:

1) As a story – just sitting down with a book of the Bible and reading it through.

2) Studying it – getting a helpful commentary online or from the bookshop and going through a bit of Scripture each day.

3) Meditating on it – just taking one verse, writing it down on a scrap of paper and then chewing on it (mentally not literally) throughout the day.

What would you say to a Christian who is struggling to read the Bible?

Me too! Reading the Bible can be tough, especially when we get to one of those random bits in Ezekiel. Or even when I'm in a less random bit! I'd say commit to doing it, pray about it, do it with a friend. Start with the passages that excite you – and after a while, challenge yourself with the bits you're less sure about. Another mistake I know I've made in the past is spending too long looking for some deep and hidden truth in a passage; to be honest, I find I get much more out of just focusing on the main and the plain meaning of the text.

What is your prayer for the Biblefresh initiative?

That others and I would fall more in love with Jesus as we discover him in his Word and as his Word reaches into our lives.

Andy Croft is Associate Director of Soul Survivor and co-author of *Storylines: Exploring the Themes of the Bible.*

SPOTLIGHT

Start with the passages that excite you.

DAVID DEWEY

KNOWING YOUR NIV FROM YOUR GNB

And it didst come to pass that there came down from the heavens a big black book, written by the Holy Ghost in words thou verily canst not understand too well. The King James Version of the Bible (the Authorized Version) dates from 1611. It is a treasured part of our Christian heritage and a landmark in English literature. But alongside it, there are now many modern translations of the Bible. A Christian bookshop may have a dozen or more on show. But which one to choose? Here we guide you though the maze of Bible translations.

Modern Bible versions cover a spectrum of translation approaches (see the diagram opposite). At one end are literal, word-for-word translations. These generally use more traditional Bible language: they are formal but dignified. Theological words like 'justified' are often retained.

Near the other end of the spectrum are meaning-for-meaning translations. The English will be more conversational and have an everyday feel. Sentences are generally shorter and the vocabulary simpler. A word like 'justified' might be replaced with 'made right with God' or similar. These translations are freer, but not necessarily any less accurate. Sometimes they are called 'dynamic' or 'functional' equivalence translations, as opposed to 'formal' equivalence versions.

As a rule, a meaning-for-meaning approach is easier to understand, while a word-for-word approach is better for in-depth study. Some versions fall between the two ends of the spectrum: midway translations follow a word-for-word approach in straightforward passages but adopt a meaning-for-meaning method in harder to understand places.

Some very free translations are called 'paraphrases'. These are often very expressive, but can be quirky. A paraphrase is best used alongside one of the more standard versions.

More recently, the issue of gender has led to the revision of some translations. In inclusive language versions 'brothers' becomes 'brothers and sisters'; 'forefathers' goes to 'ancestors'; 'workman' changes to 'worker'; and 'he' or 'she' becomes 'they'. Among such revisions are the NRSV and TNIV. The NCV, GNB, CEV and NLT also feature inclusive language.

Modern Bible versions cover a spectrum of translation approaches.

BIBLE

The Top 10

Apart from the venerable King James Version (Authorized Version) of 1611, here is a list of ten modern Protestant versions in use in Britain today. The first three are revisions of the KJV and fall into the word-for-word category:

1. **New Revised Standard Version (NRSV, 1989).** With inclusive language.

2. **English Standard Version (ESV, 2001).** Its cousin, but without the inclusive language.

3. **New King James Version (NKJV, 1982).** A KJV with the thee/thou language updated.

Others, not in the King James tradition, include:

4. **New International Version (NIV, 1978).** A best-selling translation, taking a middle approach between word-for-word and meaning-for-meaning.

5. **Today's NIV (TNIV, 2001).** An updated NIV, now with inclusive language.

6. **Good News Bible (GNB, 1976).** A meaning-for-meaning version. Used by children as well as adults.

7. **Contemporary English Version (CEV, 1995).** Similar to the GNB, but taking the meaning-for-meaning principle still further.

8. **New Living Translation (NLT 1996, revised 2004).** Another good meaning-for-meaning version, with expressive language. More sophisticated than the GNB or CEV.

9. **New Century Version (NCV, 1987).** Somewhere between the NIV and GNB. Several editions are aimed at teenagers. A simplified adaptation, the International Children's Bible, is good for pre-teens.

10. **The Message (1993).** A passionate and powerful paraphrase by Eugene Peterson.

Here is a chart of all these Bibles:

THE BIBLE TRANSLATION SPECTRUM

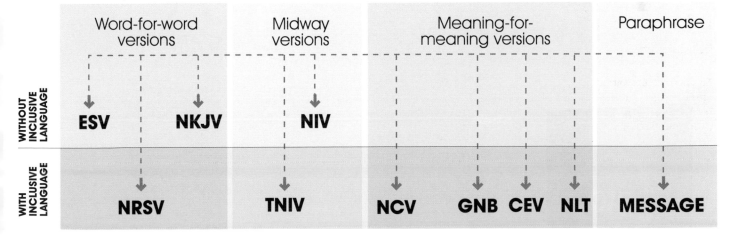

Top Tips:

- If you attend a church, find out which Bible they use. Having the same translation will make it easier to take part in Bible studies and follow sermons (perhaps!).

- Take advice from a church leader or Christian friend on which version might best suit you. A Christian bookshop can show you these in a variety of editions and prices.

- Read the preface in which the translators explain their principles, as well as how to find your way around footnotes and other features.

- Compare a passage you know well in several different versions. Many can be found on the web: www.biblegateway.com is a good place to start.

- When you come across anything in the Bible you don't understand, ask someone who might: a minister or Bible study leader.

- Ask the Holy Spirit for his help. And persevere: the more you read the Bible, the more it will make sense.

ASK THE HOLY SPIRIT FOR HIS HELP. AND PERSEVERE.

David Dewey is a Baptist minister and author of *Which Bible? A Guide to English Translations*, (IVP, 2004).

JOHN BUCKERIDGE

WHICH BIBLE?

With so many translations and paraphrases to choose from which Bible is the best? *Christianity* magazine asked a range of Christian leaders – from bishops to evangelists, pastors to scholars – what Bible translation they preferred and why. This is their response . . .

 STEVE CLIFFORD, the new General Director of the Evangelical Alliance, switched to the NIV about 20 years ago and it remains his preferred choice. 'I was persuaded as to its scholarly approach to translation – the high view with which the interpreters viewed the Scriptures – while at the same time I found it easy to read and to apply both in my own personal life and through my preaching.'

He enjoys reading other versions. '*The Message* brings a fresh and at times poetic insight to the Scriptures and I use Tom Wright's 'Everyone' series as part of my quiet times with God and find Tom's translations bring fascinating insights . . . It's amazing how God seems able to speak to us, challenging, encouraging and informing as we read the Scriptures and allow them to impact our lives.'

 MARK LANDRETH SMITH heads up a Newfrontiers church in Surrey and like Clifford uses the NIV. 'I am used to it, also it's the version most used by people in the church and, as far as I can tell, it is quite accurate. However, I often refer to and use other translations personally or when preaching. Frequently I read the same passage from *The Message* to bring further light or freshness to a passage.'

 'I am very attached to my slightly battered old, zip-up black leather NIV which I bought when I was a student 16 years ago,' says **JON KUHRT**, Community Mission Director of Livability. 'I know my way around it well, so I like the way I can easily locate stories and verses that have been particularly inspiring to me. I stick with the NIV mainly because of its familiarity and it's the version I have been mainly taught from over the years. I do find it can be too conservative in the way it interprets some passages and so it has been good to check out the NRSV, the CEV and *The Message* to get a slightly different take at times.'

 RICHARD TIPLADY, Principal of ICC, has used the NIV since coming to faith in 1985. 'When I bought a new Bible a couple of years ago, I went for the TNIV (or what the shop assistant called the 'Politically-Correct NIV'). I did this partly because of the inclusive language, but also so that I could read familiar texts with some new wording, to prevent me taking the text for granted through familiarity.'

 NOLA LEACH, Chief Executive of CARE, is another who uses the NIV, 'because I like the accuracy of the translation – as a theology graduate I like that – and the way it combines the wording I grew up with, but in a clearer way than the old RSV. However, I also love the NLT and use it often as it brings a freshness compared to the versions I know well.'

 'It seems to me the NIV has the best balance between textual integrity and good English expression of the intended meaning,' says **DAMIAN STAYNE**, the evangelist and founder of the Corinthians et Lumen Christi Roman Catholic Community in the UK. 'However the NIV does not include the Apocryphal or Deuterocanonical books which Catholic and Orthodox Churches regard as canonical. Because of this "deficiency" I tend to use two translations, the NRSV and the NJB. The NRSV because of its respect among scholars from all the major denominations, and the NJB because it has some excellent notes.'

Like the majority of the Christian leaders we spoke to, WILL VAN DER HART, Vicar of St Peter's Church in Harrow, uses the NIV preferring the Thematic Study Bible format for his sermon preparation. 'During my theology degree I became aware of the "canonical" editorial style used in the NIV which effectively works from the premise that Jesus is Lord. Obviously, I believe that to be true so it doesn't bother me that some of the Greek text is interpreted through that lens. If I was going to express a more academic preference in Bible translation it would definitely be the NRSV and I sometimes make cross reference to this translation to shed an alternative interpretation on a difficult text. If I was going to express any real frustration with the NIV it is their insertion of paragraph breaks and story titling. Neither of these things exists within the Greek text and I often sense that the editorial team has made chapter divisions or story titles that confuse the true meaning of the text. A good example is the insertion of the title and paragraph break in Ephesians 5:22 "Wives and Husbands". This single insertion separates mutual submission in verse 21 from the remainder of the text. This has then created a new and unbalanced passage which has led to many issues for women within church. Read together, the whole chapter makes much more sense!'

SHARON ANSON, a local church leader in Surrey is very keen on TNIV – the inclusive language translation which she considered a better version than the NIV.

DAVE ROBERTS, a writer and the Pastor of Living Stones Community Church, Eastbourne, is another NIV man. But he is thinking of changing to the NRSV. 'The NIV has some translation biases that N.T. Wright draws attention to in his recent book on Justification,' he explains.

PETE BROADBENT, the Bishop of Willesden and the Deputy Bishop of London gives the NRSV his thumbs up because of its 'good scholarship, accurate translation and inclusive language.' In addition 'it is commonly used in the Anglican lectionary in Common Worship and is reasonably accessible.'

ROBERT FREEMAN, the Archdeacon of Halifax, varies the Bible version he reads. 'At the moment I am reading the NRSV because I thought I ought to try reading a version that is a little more a one-to-one translation than has been my normal, and also because I found a copy going cheap at Greenbelt. When reading on a day by day basis I like to use coloured marker pencils to highlight key bits and pieces. It means my reading-Bible ends up looking rather jolly but I find it a good way of focusing in on the text and taking stock. There is a risk that the more I read the Bible the more easily I skip along through it because "I know it". Using the marker pencils slows me down and gets me thinking about what it might be saying.

'My default preference for everyday reading is the GNB. This version was the first I purchased after I became a Christian. I still have that copy complete with a tie-dyed cover made by a girlfriend. But it is not simply nostalgia or lethargy that keeps me with it. I like the clarity of expression and the way in which it seeks to make the text clear. It might not always capture the nuance of the original but what it loses in precision it gains through being immediate and vivid. It grabs me in a way that a more technical or "wordy" version might not.'

Many of the leaders we spoke to mentioned *The Message* as their second choice but GERALD COATES, the founder of the Pioneer network of new churches, makes it his number one. 'That is because I know so many sections of Scripture well – I know what's coming up – and I have found myself speed reading and almost skimming over many well known stories and passages. *The Message* slows me down quite a lot. I ask myself, "Is that what really happened? Did Jesus mean that?" or "How on earth have I missed this point (or perspective) having been a follower of Christ for 53 years?" I do use different versions when I am preparing talks and prefer some of the older translations when I am quoting passages, even if my main public reading is still from *The Message*.'

DEREK TIDBALL, former Principal of London School of Theology, uses the TNIV in public, 'because most churches I visit have the NIV in the pew. I also use it for study and my writing. In my personal devotions I use the NLT, which is a brilliant translation and should be more widely known than it is.' He accepts that the NIV/TNIV is 'a bit of a compromise' but prefers it because 'it is best known and strikes a good balance between being a more formal translation without resorting to stilted or pompous language.

'I would prefer to use the NRSV for serious work like

study and writing as it is a more "accurate" translation and is not biased in places, as the NIV is, by a confessional stance. However, its style is a bit too traditional and formal. The ESV aims for the same "literalness" of translation but suffers from the same slightly stilted English.'

As for *The Message* paraphrase, Tidball considers it 'brilliant to read' and often consults it. But considers it variable in quality – 'the translation of Colossians is superb, but in places it suffers from too many Americanisms, as in some, but not all, of the Psalms.' But he considers it is always worth looking at for its 'sheer freshness and energy'.

However Tidball's vote goes to the NLT which he 'loves – and would use it more in public if it was more widely read.'

 Author, counsellor and *Christianity* columnist MARY PYTCHES also prefers the NLT which she uses in her devotions because it is 'fresh, clear, flows easily and the language is more current. However when I am speaking I still use the NIV because I think it is still the most commonly used translation.'

 Like most of the Christian leaders we spoke to LYNDON BOWRING, the Executive Chairman of CARE, was torn when asked to choose a favourite. 'Most Scripture I've memorized is from the RSV,' he says, 'while most Scripture I preach from is the NIV.' However, like Tidball and Pytches, his favourite translation for private reading is the NLT 'which I understand to be one of the finest new translations available. It has made ancient memorized Scriptures come alive afresh for me.'

 CHARLES WHITEHEAD is a prominent charismatic Catholic and a leading figure in the annual Celebrate conference. His favourite translation is the *Jerusalem Bible*. 'The reason for this is simple and is emotional rather than academic,' he explains. 'When I came to a living faith in 1976, I spent the next few years reading, studying, devouring and enjoying the *Jerusalem Bible*. I read little else, and my copy from that time is underlined, highlighted and annotated on almost every page.

'It has long since fallen apart, and is held together with sticky tape. This Bible played a vital part in my life, and I have a huge emotional attachment to it. Today I read all the main translations, particularly the NIV, but my heart still leaps when I pick up my *Jerusalem Bible*, and a warm and comfortable feeling comes over me as I sit down and relax with this faithful old friend.'

 'In the words of Bono, "I still haven't found what I'm looking for",' says author NICK PAGE, whose books include several Bible handbooks. For him the answer is to use different translations for different purposes.

'I think it's a bit like camera lenses. The holy grail of geeky photographers is to find the single, all-purpose lens. But, in reality, they spend all their time swapping lenses on and off for different purposes: a macro lens for close-ups, a fixed lens for portraits, a zoom lens for action, etc. So here are my camera lenses:

'For in-depth Bible study, or if I'm writing a historical book, like *The Longest Week*,[1] I use the NRSV, which is accurate, but dull (it is the generally accepted translation in academic circles). For just reading the Bible, or reading aloud to others, I'll often use the CEV which has a much better feel to it and for the most part doesn't sound like it has been written by a committee of very old men with doctorates but a limited grasp of the modern world. If I want to stir things up a bit I'll use *The Message*, although I think as a translation it has severe limitations.

'And then there's the NIV. Which, frankly, if you were looking for one all-purpose lens, is your best bet by far (especially since the new edition has some rather yummy maps designed by yours truly in the end pages).

'The problem with most translations,' according to Page 'is that they are all written' by committees. The translation committee makes sure everything sounds the same. It's a flattening device. That's why *The Message* stands out. It has a personality. Too many Bible translations manage to take the exciting, passionate word of God and make it sound like an EU Directive on the Quality Control of Cabbages. What we need are more translators who can capture the literary style of the original – who can capture the excitement of Paul, the anger of Jeremiah, the sheer full-on, in-your-face shock tactics of Ezekiel. The Bible is actually more varied, more exciting, more rude, more moving, more weird and wonderful than we think. But you don't get weird, wonderful, moving, exciting, rude, varied writing from a committee!'

 'I use the anglicized version of the NRSV for study and private devotions,' says DAVID COFFEY, President of the Baptist World Alliance and former General Secretary of the Baptist Union and Moderator of the Free Churches. 'It is one of the best cross-reference Bibles in print and is the nearest version in style to the RSV which I used when I was being formed in discipleship classes and later in theological college. I love the rhythm of the NRSV and enjoy reading aloud from this version.

But because most of the UK churches I speak in request the NIV or the TNIV, this is the version I use for preaching.'

MERVYN THOMAS is the Chief Executive of Christian Solidarity Worldwide that works with persecuted Christians around the world. He uses the NASV and has done for about twenty-five years. 'I find it particularly useful in sermon preparation,' he says and claims, 'it is normally regarded as the most literally translated of the twentieth century English translations. Although I am not normally a fan of all things American I have found the NASV to be very close to the King James (which I grew up on and love dearly) but nevertheless a little more understandable.'

'I tend to use several versions of the Bible fairly indiscriminately,' admits **ERIC DELVE** of St Luke's Church, Maidstone. 'My daily Bible readings take place in the one-year Bible I have which is the NLT. Like many, I have for many years used the NIV but have to confess that its rather conservative use of language and focus on a religious mindset makes it not the happiest translation from which to preach, though I do frequently use it. I still find great stimulus from reading the NRSV. I was actually brought up of course in an era when the RSV was the version of choice amongst many evangelicals. When the NIV came out, David Pawson took to calling it the Nearly Ideal Version and the RSV the Recently Superseded Version. I love *The Message* and frequently find it stimulating and refreshing. I often use *The Message* and the NLT as public reading versions in church and to preach from.

'Now and again when recalling some beloved passage from my childhood, I revert to the NKJV. On balance I would guess that the version I most commonly use is probably still the NIV, though the NLT and *The Message* run very close.

'I feel so blessed that we have so many different versions which give us access to hidden treasures.'

It seems that while most of the leaders we spoke to have a preferred version, variety is the spice of life – and switching translations helps keep Scripture fresh. So whatever version you usually read, try swapping to another to keep the important spiritual discipline of Scripture alive.

Bible Translations mentioned in this article are:

ESV	English Standard Version
GNB	Good News Bible
NIV	New International Version
NASV	New American Standard Version
NKJV	New King James Version
NJB	New Jerusalem Bible
NLT	New Living Translation
NRSV	New Revised Standard Version
RSV	Revised Standard Version
TNIV	Today's New International Version
	The Message

John Buckeridge is Editor of *Christianity* magazine.

Taken from *Christianity* magazine (August, 2009). Used by permission. www.christianitymagazine.co.uk

I feel so blessed that we have so many different versions which give us access to hidden treasures.

BLESSED

MATT VALLER

BOOK GROUP

It's 7.55 p.m. On a beach somewhere in Cornwall, five friends prepare to surf under the late-summer sunset. One has a Bible in hand. They read the story of Peter getting out of the boat to meet Jesus. And with the words ringing in their ears they take the plunge and carve their way across the waves.

Meanwhile, hundreds of miles away, Martin and Daryl arrive at the King's Head for their weekly discussion over a pint. They are reading the whole Bible again this year. 'It's just so helpful to do this every week,' says Martin, a retired project manager. 'I've learnt so much about the Bible just by talking it through with someone else.'

Reading the Bible in groups is hardly a new idea. But fresh creativity is capturing worn-out students of the Scriptures; people of all ages are forging new rhythms of reading and finding new meaning in the most unlikely of places.

'We take typical biblical stories, but approach them in unorthodox ways', explains Michael, who runs Stage-Fright, a Bible-reading theatre club for young people. 'We're trying to break the laziness that comes with hearing the same story told in the same way over and over again. By actively telling the story each person is participating in it, rather than being an audience; they have no option but to engage their own thoughts.'

Rachel took a similar approach with her youth group. 'In one session we asked each person to make a model city out of cardboard and imaginatively describe the people who lived there. Then we read parts of the story of Joshua from the Bible and one by one their model cities were destroyed. It was a way of reading the story from the other side. These young people had grown up in church and known about a great victory for Joshua; they had never stopped to think from the perspective of the Canaanites.

'Reading this way threw up all kinds of important questions about God and power which we were able to explore together', explains Rachel. 'When you read with other people you don't just hear other points of view; you have the potential to experience the reading in a dynamic and provocative way that is all but impossible on your own.'

For Dan, of 24-7 Prayer, it's getting to grips with the story as a whole that's made all the difference. 'The Bible isn't a self-help book or a horoscope; it's a collection of stories that form part of a larger story of what God is doing in the world,' he explains. 'It's God's story, so reading is about us finding our place in that, rather than the other way around.

'For us, reading the Bible as a story has really connected with people, particularly people who have struggled with reading it in the past. You don't need a degree in theology – it frees people from the burden of reading the Bible; they can enjoy it again; they can get caught up in the story.

'I think the Bible is *meant* to be read and understood with others. I was taught as a kid that you read your Bible in your quiet time, but I think the Bible has so much more – for groups of people, for churches, for house groups, for sharing with your friends. That's how the best stories are retold.'

Reading the Bible together is not just for Christians either. For twenty-something Andy, reading the Bible with people who have no Christian background has been an exciting journey. 'I ran a football team,' he explains, 'and I challenged them to find out more about my faith. They didn't want to come to church. But they would come to the pub! So we started reading the Bible together there.'

For Andy and his friends, the Bible is an unpredictable read. 'Often people will ask things that I've never really thought about,' he says. 'They are coming to each passage without any previous experience of reading it and stuff will jump out at them which I would have just passed over. But it feels really liberating to read this way; we just see what questions come out, rather than me imposing my questions on the group from above.'

Sharing Bible-reading experiences with others has always been a sacred practice. In coffee shops, pubs and beaches, with novices, veterans and the disillusioned, people – young and old – are opening up the Scriptures together; readers of the Story of Stories are making provocative steps towards finding their place in the plotline.

The surfers were doing **Lyfe** together, a resource from Bible Society that connects Bible reading with everyday culture. To find out more visit www.lyfe.org.uk

24-7 Prayer run a year-long training programme of which Bible reading is an integral part. For more information visit www.24-7prayer.com/learning

To find out more about the work of **Stage-Fright** visit www.stage-fright.org.uk

Andy set up **Be Church.** Visit their blog at www.be-church.org

I THINK THE BIBLE IS MEANT TO BE READ AND UNDERSTOOD WITH OTHERS.

Matt Valler is National Youthwork Co-ordinator for Tearfund.

PETE PHILLIPS

WHAT'S THE BIBLE EVER DONE FOR ME?

At a particularly difficult time in his ministry, Jesus gave his disciples the opportunity to jump ship. Instead, Peter turned to Jesus and said 'Lord, where shall we go? You have the words of eternal life.'

Now, I know that Peter didn't necessarily mean that Jesus' words and the words of the Bible were synonymous. However, I think it is OK to see the phrase referring both to the words of Jesus and the words which are contained in the Bible – both Jesus, the Word of God incarnate, and the Bible, the written Word of God. It means stretching the meaning a little because when Peter spoke those words, he only knew Jesus and the Old Testament but, in the longer perspective of what God is doing, I think my version stands.

I had found the Bible to be life-enriching even before I became a Christian. I enjoyed its message of life and community and, as a tearaway socialist teenager, I loved its revolutionary, world-changing ideology. Here was a message of justice and passion. The Bible was also good in arguments and I soon found myself 'inside' the Christian groups although not really aware of what being a Christian meant. While I was exploring the Christian faith in sixth form, I realized the Bible 'spoke' to me in lots of different ways – through the words themselves, through preachers, through my friends. When it was time to make a decision, it was the Bible that showed me the way – through a fantastic exploration of the vine imagery in John 15. Because of that passage, and lots of my friends' patient debating, I became a Christian. And then, the morning after I became a Christian, I found myself drawn to Colossians 3:1 which begins 'Since, then, you have been raised with Christ . . .' I didn't know that verse before that moment but it seemed so right and summed up my own experience of the night before and guided me into the next stages of living out that Christian life.

I've used the Bible throughout my life since, as a Christian, as a preacher, minister and teacher. I have found at times that it is too easy to become a professional Bible user – to take God's Word for granted, to feel that Bible study is the same as Bible research. But I know how important it is to allow the Bible to have its say within my life. Or, if you prefer, to let the Holy Spirit bring the Bible to life again and again and again within my life. That means putting in time to let the Bible speak rather than just seeing it as a study tool or as an object of research. It means consciously standing under the Bible rather than always hovering over it as a New Testament scholar. Again and again I have found that it is the Bible that has spoken into a situation to bring comfort, challenge, guidance and hope.

So, I wasn't surprised that when something pretty nasty happened at work and we realized it was time to move on, it was through the Bible that God encouraged us and guided us on our way. 'I have watched over you and have seen what has been done to you in Egypt. And I have promised to bring you up out of your misery . . . [to] a land flowing with milk and honey.' The verses (Exodus 3:1-17, NIV) refer to an ancient journey much more important than our own. They refer to specific places, which are not relevant to us. However, spoken

into our context and our situation, they provided such a sense of peace and direction – God was with us and understood our journey and would bless us on our way.

I have to say that throughout my Christian life, the Bible continues to speak into my existence, guiding, leading, encouraging, challenging. It's not magic and I don't go round opening my Bible at random passages to see what God has to say about something. It's an awareness of the Bible guided by the Holy Spirit, which has borne out Peter's words that what Jesus offers to us are the words of eternal life. In the chaos and confusion of my life, of all our lives, I need those words so much.

> I have to say that throughout my Christian life, the Bible speaks into my existence.

EXISTENCE

Pete Phillips is Director of Research at the Centre for Biblical Literacy and Communication, St John's College, Durham University.

CODEC

GROW WITH THE BIBLE

WHAT KIND OF BIBLE READER ARE YOU ?

Bible reading can be a bit hit or miss for many of us. Most of us aspire to read the Bible every day but end up feeling guilty when we fail. We know it is in the Bible that we meet God, draw closer to him, learn about his purposes for our lives, find resources for living and ministry and have our lives transformed. But where to start, and how to keep going?

I have been experimenting with a 'seven-a-week' approach to Bible reading, modelled on the 'five-a-day' fruit and vegetable campaign. I really want to eat five bits of fruit and veg a day, but don't feel guilty when I don't manage it. For me it's an aspirational goal rather than a guilt-inducing target. 'Seven-a-week', recognizes that some of us don't manage to get a daily time reading the Bible so we binge read at the weekends when time can be a little easier to find.

Realistically, we are more likely to stay on track reading the Bible if we take a systematic approach, rather than just reading our favourite bits. A system will provide motivation and keep us going when it gets tough. And it can be useful to have some notes to help us make sense of the Bible reading and apply it to our lives.

There's a wealth of material to help you on this exciting journey. But the choice can be somewhat daunting. How do you know what is best for you? To get you thinking, why not try this simple questionnaire. It's not foolproof, but may give you a way in . . .

1 You are given a new gadget. Do you:

a) Read the instructions before you switch it on
b) Immediately give it a go
c) Observe someone else using it and follow their lead
d) Think about how you want to make your life easier

2 In terms of connecting with God, you naturally prefer:

a) Structured liturgy
b) Alternative and experimental worship
c) Quiet meditative prayer
d) Praying with friends in a small group

3 When going on a journey, do you:

a) Read the map and plan your journey in advance
b) Set out and hope for the best
c) Work out the route by recalling how you travelled this way before
d) Punch the postcode into the sat nav and away you go

4 Your ideal evening out is:

a) A robust debate with a few friends
b) Non-stop dancing
c) A trip to the cinema
d) Helping out with a friend's DIY or craft project

5 Given a limited choice on TV, you would opt for:

a) Question Time
b) Bear Grylls or another 'real life' programme
c) An arts or natural history documentary
d) Grand Designs

6 You would prefer to listen to:

a) Radio 4
b) Radio 1
c) Classic FM
d) Spotify or LastFM

SCORES:

Mostly As - You are a Regulator
Mostly Bs - You are a Builder
Mostly Cs - You are an Architect
Mostly Ds - You are a Surveyor

REGULATORS thrive with structure and enjoy working systematically

BUILDERS want to jump in, get hands-on and try things out for themselves

ARCHITECTS enjoy taking a step back to examine the bigger picture

SURVEYORS want something that they can test for its practical value

There are resources to help you read the Bible with others (virtually or in small groups), as well as by yourself: both are valuable. This list is not exhaustive, but hopefully will inspire you to try something to suit your learning style.

PERSONAL

COMMUNAL

REGULATOR →

Search the Scriptures (IVP)
Provides a systematic course of daily Bible study, using the NIV translation.

Cover to Cover (CWR)
Created to bring in-depth biblical understanding to 'thinking Christians'. Constructed on a five-year rolling plan, which takes you through the entire Bible, book by book.

Encounter with God (Scripture Union)
A thorough and energetic investigation of the whole Bible, complemented by pastoral warmth from a strong field of writers and contributors. New features provide insights into Christian spirituality, tackle contemporary issues, and profile inspiring teachers.

Guidelines (BRF)
For more in-depth study, this contains continuous commentary on Bible passages, with introductions and background information, arranged in weekly units. Contributors are leading scholars from around the world, representing a thought-provoking breadth of Christian tradition.

Foundations 21 (BRF)
A resource for discipleship and lifelong Christian learning. It explores twelve key building blocks of the Christian faith – including prayer, the cross and mission – with a flexible blend of web-based study, group interaction and personal application. *Foundations 21* establishes and builds on firm foundations for spiritual growth, with increasing levels of depth (www.foundations21.org.uk).

BUILDER →

Living Light (Nationwide Christian Trust)
Daily Bible reflections published on a quarterly basis. Each week a Bible passage is focused on, with a verse per day from within that passage explored in more depth.

New Daylight (BRF)
Offers four months of daily Bible reading and reflection, ideal for those looking for a devotional approach to reading and understanding the Bible. Each reading includes the Bible passage, a comment from the contributor and a prayer or reflection.

Word for the Week (LICC)
Free weekly email from the London Institute for Contemporary Christianity, with a brief, but profound, comment on a Bible passage, earthed in real-life contexts and accompanying questions for reflection.

Archive of reflections include a series on how whole-life discipleship is an integral part of the gospel and is woven through Scripture as a whole, from creation to new creation, from the garden of Genesis to the city of Revelation (www.licc.org.uk/engagin-with-the-bible/word-of-the-week).

Essential 100 (Scripture Union)
A church-wide Bible reading programme built around a carefully selected list of short Bible passages. It enables people to get the big picture of the Bible without getting bogged down in some of the more detailed descriptive chapters.

ARCHITECT →

The Bible for Everyone (SPCK)
A major series of guides to all the books of the New Testament by N.T. Wright. These include Wright's own fresh translation of the entire text. Each short passage is followed by a highly readable discussion with background information.

Deo Vox (Damaris)
A 4–6 minute audio dive into the Bible, both downloadable and a podcast. It includes a passage from the Bible, followed by commentary, plus movie clips to relate the Bible to life (www.damaris.org/cm/home/deovox).

Closer to God (Scripture Union)
Designed to help you listen to the Holy Spirit as you approach the Scriptures. Contains a Bible reading with notes for every day of the week, but with allowance for missing a couple of studies per week, without getting behind. Also includes prayer, praise and reflection.

Community of Readers (LICC)
Receive a weekly email with the up-coming reading plan, plus short comment from different authors on each of the week's Old and New Testament readings. You can engage with other readers, discussing the themes thrown up by the different passages, and offer your own perspectives into the mix. Community of Readers is born from the idea that the Bible is meant to be shared and that by reading and engaging together we open our ears to the whispers of God (www.communityofreaders.com).

The Word for Today (UCB)
Daily Bible readings for the year, available in paper format, email or podcast, exploring the Bible alongside contemporary themes and issues. Readings and prayers come from writers from different cultures, which challenge readers to think and act in new ways (www.ucb.co.uk/word_for_today).

you take some time to absorb it. You could ask yourself:

- If my life was gripped by what I've read what difference would it make?
- Do I feel this is true for me? (Don't just give it a mental tick.)
- What comfort and what challenges does it bring me?

9. BIBLE HELP

There are all sorts of commentaries, Bible notes and study guides that can really help us as we read the Bible. They can ask us questions and so get us thinking, and they can explain difficult bits so we understand. My tip is - vary the sort of help you get. Don't always use guides that 'tell you the answer' - otherwise you won't think for yourself. But don't always use guides which only ask questions - otherwise you can end up feeling stuck. Do a bit of both!

10. BIBLE PRAYER

Relationships are two-way things. If only one person talks it's a bit weird. So as we read the Bible, and experience God speaking to us, the most natural response should be to speak back to him. We can pray all sorts of things:

- I don't get this bit, would you help me understand your Word?
- What you're saying is really challenging, please help me trust you and accept it.
- You are amazing - look at what you're like and what you've done!

Let the Bible lead you to pray.

Nigel Beynon is Director of New Word Alive and co-author of *Dig Deeper* (IVP, 2005).

new word alive
Serving the Church, Reaching the World

FRESHEN UP

10 BIBLE READING IDEAS FOR YOUR CHURCH **KRISH KANDIAH**

Reading the Bible is vital for personal spiritual growth, but reading the Bible together is an equally important discipline. Most of the time in the New Testament letters, when we read the word 'you' it is not addressing us as individuals, but as a company of God's people. Seeing the Bible as a corporate resource bonds believers better together, builds stronger churches, and unites us with other Christians throughout history and across the globe. Here are some ideas to bring the Bible back into the centre of our corporate worship.

1. BIBLE IN A YEAR

Many of us have never managed to read the Bible cover to cover and there are large chunks of the Bible that are uncharted territory. How about committing yourselves - as a whole church, a house group, prayer triplet or a family - to read the whole Bible through in a year. Having others 'jogging at the same pace' alongside you can encourage you to persist when the going gets tough. There are lots of different resources to help you do this:

- Join a community of readers - or create your own through Facebook or your church website - and together set passages and discuss what you're discovering.
- Buy a 'one-year Bible' divided into 365 daily readings with dates.
- Follow a simple plan to read three chapters of the Old Testament and one chapter of the New Testament each day.
- Get hold of the new *NIV Soul Survivor Bible in One Year (Hodder & Stoughton, 2010)* which has been specially produced for young people to read the Bible during the academic year, with plenty of online help.
- Listen to the day's reading online at: http://m.enewhope.org/bible

2. BIBLE ALOUD

The invention of the printing press in the mid-fifteenth century made it possible for Bibles to be owned rather than remembered, but it is only in the past 150 years that the Bible has been cheap enough for the average family in the UK to own one. Before then, the Word of God was largely heard read aloud. When Ezra read out the Law for eight days straight it led to an enormous change in God's people. King Josiah did the same in his day, leading to repentance and revival. There is a special promise of blessing for those who hear the book of Revelation read aloud. Imagine we recapture that experience of listening to God's Word together, expecting God to speak, move and bless.

An initiative similar to the 24/7 prayer weeks that have been adopted by many churches could see a 24/7 week of public Bible reading, where Christians take shifts in reading Scripture aloud, as other people drop by to listen and meditate.

3. BIBLE RELAY

An alternative twist to Bible Aloud would see a single Bible being read cover to cover publicly by a group of local churches in consecutive weeks. Post-it notes on the relevant pages could be used to allow listeners to respond and by the end of the year the messages could be collated, to see what God is saying to his churches in that area.

4. RESPECTING GOD'S WORDS

One way we can help our congregations to value God's Word more is to show greater respect when it is read. This could simply mean offering a prayer to God before the public reading of the Bible in the church service. You could encourage those who are able to, to stand or kneel as a sign that we are being addressed by God.

Perhaps asking people to fold their hands and close their eyes as a sign of submission would convey a sense of respect through body language.

5. BIBLE MEMORIZE

When I was 14 years old my pastor asked me to memorize Isaiah chapter six, so that I could recite it in church before he preached from that passage. Despite being nervous, I worked hard to get it exactly right and deliver it with passion and emotion. You could have heard a pin drop as the congregation was transfixed on hearing God's Word. Not only did the occasion transform what was normally a pretty perfunctory part of the church service, but it had a significant impact on my own life too. It gave me an appetite to memorize Scripture and 25 years later, I can still remember that text more or less word for word. I would encourage churches to look for some willing volunteers to bless their congregations in this way during the Biblefresh year.

6. READ THE BIBLE IN ANOTHER LANGUAGE

If your church includes people from different cultures, why not have the Bible read aloud in different languages representing those that are present in the service. People can follow in English on the screen. Hearing the Bible in another language can force you to read your own more closely – and for those whose first language is not English, it sends a powerful message that the Word of God is equally at home in their mother tongue. Alternatively, reading the Bible in a different translation can again force listeners out of their auto-shutdown mode when the Bible is being read.

7. BYOB

If Sunday is the only day that some of us read the Bible, and even then only as a projected script, it is possible that many Christians won't touch a Bible for months. Some churches have stopped putting out pew Bibles or projecting the text in a bid to encourage Christians to carry their own Bibles around, to remember how to look up references and to get used to seeing a text in its context – scanning what comes before and after the part that is being preached on. One pastor I heard about realized that his congregation was unfamiliar with the Bible as a book and spent a whole service preaching from the contents page, showing how the books fitted together. Another church encouraged members at the beginning of the year to touch, smell and feel the Bible and to give thanks for the sweat, tears and blood that were shed to get the Bible to us in the first place. Perhaps denote one Sunday a month as BYOB (Bring your own Bible) and offer to give Bibles away that week to visitors who don't have their own.

8. ONLINE COMMUNITY

Lots of us spend time online each day for work and leisure. Although the online community may not have the warmth of face-to-face encounters, by reading the same material as others in your congregation, you are in some way brought together. This is particularly valuable for those who are housebound or for those who travel away from home for work. Perhaps as a church you could agree to use one of the following:

- Youversion (www.youversion.com)
- Foundations21 (www.foundations21.org.uk)
- Wordlive (www.scriptureunion.org.uk/wordlive)

9. BOOK GROUP

Whether you are part of a secular book group, inter-church Lent house group, *Just Looking* course, or another reading group, why not suggest exploring a book of the Bible together? My experience of doing this has been very exciting, as I watched people come to the Bible with freshness and vitality and help those over-familiar with the text, rediscover the power and beauty of God's Word within.

10. READING MENTORS

Some Christians find having a mentor or spiritual director a really helpful way to grow in their faith. During the Biblefresh year, you could encourage people in church to get together with someone they trust and respect in the faith for a six-week trial period. Prior to meeting, both parties would commit to studying a whole book of the Bible together and then discuss and pray about the things that they had learned. A book like *One to One: A Discipleship Handbook* by Sophie de Witt might help you to get started.

Krish Kandiah is Executive Director: Churches in Mission at the Evangelical Alliance and author of *Dysciples: Why I fall asleep when I pray, and twelve other discipleship dysfunctions* (Authentic, 2009).

wake up read Galatians 5:22

breakfast meeting

stuck in traffic

remember Galatians 5:22

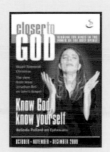

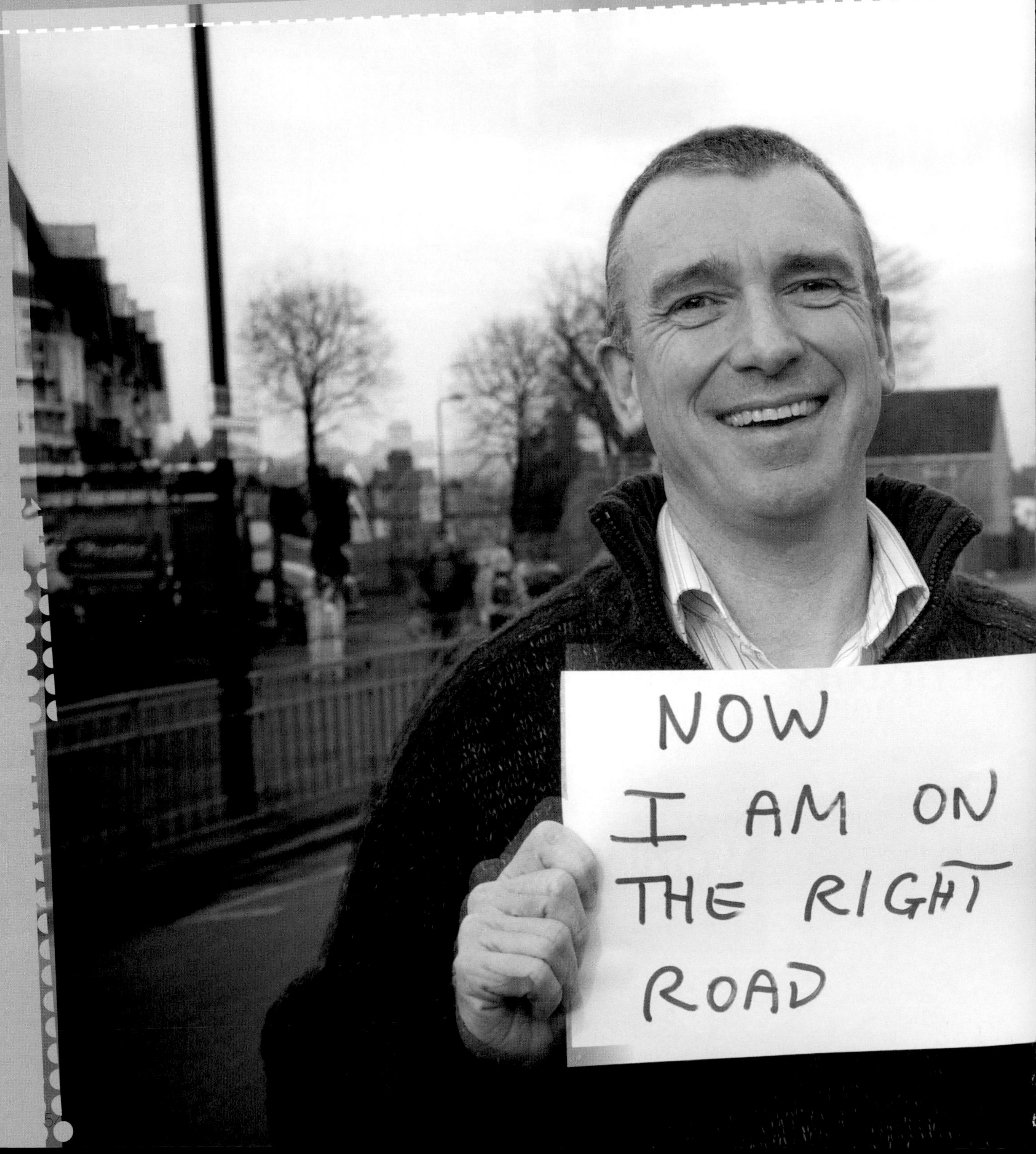
NOW
I AM ON
THE RIGHT
ROAD

HONING YOUR SKILLS

BIBLE TRAINING

VAUGHAN ROBERTS

THE BIG PICTURE OF THE BIBLE

An Australian friend recently went on a ten-day coach tour around Western Europe. The pace of travel might have put me off tourism for life, but it whetted my friend's appetite. He gained an overview of the geography of Western Europe and some of its attractions, which made him determined to return for a much more detailed look another time. I hope this brief article will have a similar effect on you. My aim is to take you on a whistle-stop tour of the whole Bible in about seven hundred words. Many have found that once they see the big picture of how all sixty-six books fit together, parts of the Bible which had previously seemed irrelevant begin to make sense.

The Bible is not just a human book, written by many different authors at different times in history, it is also a divine book, inspired by the Holy Spirit. That explains why it fits together as a unity; ultimately, it is one book with one divine author and one great subject: God's plan to save the world through his Son Jesus Christ. The story of the Bible can be summarized in four words: Creation, Fall, Promise and Fulfilment.

1. CREATION (Genesis 1 - 2)
God creates human beings and gives them authority, under him, over the wonderful world he had made.

2. FALL (Genesis 3)
Adam and Eve rebel against God's rightful authority and, ever since, their descendants seek to live independently of him. The results are disastrous, not just for human beings, but for the whole created order. Instead of enjoying an intimate relationship with God, humanity is now under his judgement.

3. PROMISE (Genesis 12 - 15)
In God's amazing love he is determined to put things right again. He promises Abraham that his descendants will be his own people; both enjoying blessing from him themselves and also being a means of his blessing to all nations. This promise is the gospel, which is partially fulfilled in the history of Israel, but is finally fulfilled through Jesus Christ.

OT PROMISE → FULFILMENT NT

a) Promise: Old Testament history (Exodus to 2 Chronicles)

The history books of the Bible tell the story of how God's promises are partially fulfilled in the history of Israel. The book of Exodus describes how the Israelites are set apart from the other nations when God rescues them from slavery in Egypt, reveals his law to them on Mount Sinai and lives in their midst in a special tent, the Tabernacle. He then gives them the land of Canaan (Joshua), provides leaders for them, of whom the greatest are David and Solomon (1 and 2 Samuel, 1 Kings) and replaces the Tabernacle with a magnificent temple.

b) Promise: Old Testament prophecy (Isaiah to Malachi)

Despite all that God did for them, the Israelites continued to disobey him so he judged them, as the prophets foretold. The northern tribes were destroyed by the Assyrians and then the people of Judah were taken into exile by the Babylonians (2 Kings). But God promised through the prophets that there was hope beyond this judgement: one day he would send a perfect King, his Son, to bring salvation.

In God's amazing love he is determined to put things right again.

4. FULFILMENT (New Testament)

a) Jesus on earth (the Gospels)

Jesus Christ demonstrated in his life, teaching and miracles that he was who he claimed to be: God's divine Son who had come, as the prophets foretold, to bring salvation. On the cross he took the punishment that sinful human beings deserved so that those who trust in him need not face God's judgement but can come back into relationship with him. He rose from the dead, ascended into heaven and now reigns over the whole of creation.

b) The last days (Acts to Revelation)

Jesus taught that there would be a delay between his first and second comings so that people from all nations can hear the good news about his salvation, put their trust in him and be ready when he returns. God sent his Holy Spirit on the day of Pentecost so that all Christians can know his presence with them and be equipped as his witnesses.

c) The new creation (Revelation 21 - 22)

When Jesus returns he will judge those who continue to reject his rule and remove all that spoils the world. He will then establish a perfectly restored new creation in which his people will enjoy life in his presence, in harmony with one another and the world. Then, at last, all God's promises will be fulfilled and we will praise him eternally for his amazing grace.

Vaughan Roberts is Rector of St Ebbe's, Oxford, Director of the Proclamation Trust and author of *God's Big Picture* (IVP, 2009).

Vaughan Roberts

God's Big Picture

Tracing the storyline of the Bible

MIKE PILAVACHI & ANDY CROFT

STORYLINES:
TRACING THREADS THAT RUN THROUGH THE BIBLE

The prophetic book of Ezekiel is one of the wackiest in the Bible. We meet wheels within wheels, chariots of fire and a man who passes 390 days lying on one side, in addition to shaving all his hair off in order to perform different crazy but symbolic acts with it . . . we can understand why Ezekiel might be thought to be one sandwich short of the full picnic. However, the book of Ezekiel is a key to a deeper understanding of the meaning of the glorious presence of our God.

Ezekiel received his visions while with the Israelites in exile in Babylon. In chapter 10 Ezekiel has a vision in which he's transported to the Temple back in Jerusalem. In the Temple he is shown four horrendous scenes. They are different scenes of the people of Israel worshipping idols and they highlight how Israel is sinning on the very doorstep of God's house. The last and worst act Ezekiel is shown is in the inner court of the Temple, just outside the sanctuary of God. Here there are 25 men, with their backs to the sanctuary, prostrating themselves and worshipping the sun. The seriousness, scale and shame of this sin is huge. Imagine returning home to find not only that your wife or husband is committing adultery, but that, disgustingly, they've been having sex in the bed the two of you are meant to share . . . Israel's repeated sin penetrated even to the most sacred of places. The holy God had longed to dwell with his people. Since their time in Egypt, Israel had been repeatedly turning away from God. He had sent them warning after warning, prophet after prophet, trying and trying to call his rebellious people back to him.

The holy God, the God who kept himself separate from all that was unholy, had set aside the Temple as his dwelling place. It is no coincidence that when describing Israel's sin Ezekiel repeatedly uses the phrase 'to profane' – the opposite of 'to make holy' (the word 'profane' in Ezekiel makes up 39 of its 71 appearances in the Bible).

It is often the holy name of God that is described as being profaned, and in one striking phrase God himself announces, 'You have profaned me' (Ezekiel 13:19). Ezekiel's vision tells us that even the corner among his people that God had claimed as holy ground was being used to worship other gods. In effect his home, the place on earth where he had chosen to dwell, had, in a spiritual sense, been broken into, spat on, defiled, trampled over and scorned.

The holy God could no longer dwell in such a place and so, reluctantly but without a choice, he packed his bags and he left his home among his people. In Ezekiel's vision he sees the glory of the Lord depart from the Temple. The glory hovers at the edge of the Temple; it's as if God is having one last look around before he finally leaves (Ezekiel 10). It is because the holiness of God is offended that the glory of God leaves.

God's address was no longer in Jerusalem and this proved to have disastrous consequences. The people of Israel, just before Jerusalem was destroyed, thought their city was indestructible. How could anyone come close to conquering Jerusalem – it was where God lived! In 586 BC the king of Babylon crushed the city and destroyed the Temple. This would have sent shockwaves throughout Israel – the place where God lived had been conquered! Ezekiel would have agreed that the place God chose to live in was indestructible. The point was he no longer lived in Jerusalem! The presence of God had left the Temple.

The presence will return . . . eventually

Having predicted the fall of Jerusalem, Ezekiel went on to prophesy about the day Israel would return from exile. In Ezekiel 40-48 he has a vision of a new Temple being built and the glory of the Lord returning to dwell among his people. This vision carries echoes of the paradise of Eden; a river is seen flowing from the south side of the altar in the Temple. In the Bible water is symbolic of life and particularly the Holy Spirit. It's when the presence of the living God returns to the Temple that life returns to Israel.

As the river flows out from the Temple in the vision, the dry, parched, barren, dead land becomes rich, abundant, and overflows with goodness. Ezekiel tells us that 'where the river flows everything will live' (Ezekiel 47:9, NIV). Furthermore he prophesies that this sanctuary is to surpass the old one; the Lord intends to 'put my sanctuary among them for ever. My dwelling-place will be with them; I will be their God, and they will be my people. Then the nations will know that I the LORD make Israel holy, when my sanctuary is among them for ever' (Ezekiel 37:26-28).

Eventually the people of Israel started to return from exile. One of the first things they did was begin to rebuild the Temple at Jerusalem. This is recorded in the book of Ezra and Nehemiah. Ezra tells us that those who remembered the old Temple wept when they saw the new one being built:

> **All the people gave a great shout of praise to the LORD, because the foundation of the house of the LORD was laid. But many of the older priests and Levites and family heads, who had seen the former temple, wept aloud when they saw the foundation of this temple being laid, while many others shouted for joy.**
> (Ezra 3:11-12, NIV)

Why did they weep? Nobody knows for sure. It could have been that the new Temple was much smaller and plainer than the old Temple; it could have been that they just didn't like the colour scheme. It could have been, however, that the older priests who remembered the first Temple realized that

something was missing, or rather Someone: this time there is no account of God manifesting his presence.

In our travels we have visited some churches that have made our mouths water because of all the stuff they have: sound systems that would be an engineer's dream; lighting that wouldn't look out of place at Wembley; soft, comfortable chairs; coffee shops and slick presentations. And yet, to be honest, sometimes we've been bored. Then we've sometimes been to other churches where, as we've walked through the door, we've thought, 'This place could do with a coat of paint and a bit of air freshener.' Yet as the meeting has started it's impossible not to recognize it: the manifest presence of God. When God shows up people don't care how hard the seats are! This is not to say we haven't encountered the manifest presence of God in some very nice buildings . . . the point is that the presence of God, not the building, matters. The dedication of this new Temple in Ezra 6 is different. The glory fell at the dedication of the Tabernacle in the wilderness; it fell at the dedication of the first Temple under Solomon; yet it is notably absent in the dedication of the second Temple. But what of Ezekiel's visions? Didn't he predict that the glory would return? Didn't he tell us that a river of life would flow? Perhaps the older priests were thinking he had got it wrong . . . Enter Jesus.

Taken from *Storylines* by Mike Pilavachi and Andy Croft (Survivor Books, 2008). Used by permission.

Mike Pilavachi is co-founder and leader of Soul Survivor and Pastor of Soul Survivor church in Watford.

STORYLINES

ANDY CROFT AND MIKE PILAVACHI

Andy Croft is Associate Director of Soul Survivor.

SOUL SURVIVOR

Living the lyfe

lyfe is a new way of engaging with the Bible. It's about meeting with your friends in a public place (coffee shop/pub/restaurant), to connect God, you and everyday life. It's about encountering the Bible with your heart and mind, in a fresh and vital way.

Using material downloaded from a dedicated website, groups follow a three-step process of engaging with a particular biblical text. By reading, reflecting and then responding to what they've encountered, the group approaches the Bible afresh.

Find out more at lyfe.org.uk

lyfe **B**

Christina Baxter

Tell us about a time when God spoke to you vividly and personally through the Bible.

When I was about 15, I was looking for a verse in the book of Joshua, which actually comes in the last chapter, but the Lord spoke to me through Joshua 1:7–8 – and called me to study theology. This has been my life's work, and it all started by reading the Bible.

In recent years what has helped to keep the Bible fresh for you?

Two things: reading it every day with other people in college chapel or small group and reading and pondering it in depth in a monthly quiet day or yearly retreat.

What does your regular practice of Bible reading look like?

As well as the things mentioned above, I read the Scriptures in private times of quiet daily and on other occasions take the chance to study it in depth, with good commentaries.

What would you say to a Christian who is struggling to read the Bible?

I'd say:
1. Ask God to help you.
2. Get a good translation.
3. Try reading in different ways – use the same psalm every day for a week and perhaps learn it off by heart. If you read short passages usually, give yourself a longer passage – why not read the whole of the book of Ruth, for instance, at once?
4. Ask other people to help you.
5. Find a good set of Bible reading notes.
6. Focus on the parts you find easiest to understand and ask God to lead you to other more difficult passages when you are ready.

What is your prayer for the Biblefresh initiative?

I am praying the Bible may be read throughout the church, so all Christians can help their neighbours who are seeking faith, to find Jesus.

I read the Scriptures in private times of quiet daily and on other occasions take the chance to study it in depth.

Christina Baxter is Principal of St John's College, Nottingham and the author of *The Wounds of Jesus* (Zondervan, 2005).

SPOTLIGHT

ROGER FORSTER

WHEN THERE'S NO
'HELP' BUTTON

Some while ago, a minister told of his experience in studying the Scriptures. He had seen my wide-margin Bible full of notes and coloured underlinings. With great expectation he bought a set of multicoloured pens and sat down in front of his open Bible. In his words, 'nothing happened'. He got up after half an hour with an unmarked Bible and an empty head. Of course I'm sorry about that failure but I don't want to leave you in the same state. So what's missing? Concordance!

Now a concordance is the product of Bible lovers and scholars collating alphabetically all the words of the Bible, showing their Greek, Hebrew and Aramaic roots (origins). By this we can find very quickly a word, its verse and those verses where there is agreement. Concordance means 'agreement'.

Someone might say: 'I thought the Holy Spirit would help me to understand the Bible he has written' (cf. Timothy 3:16). It is true, says Jesus: 'The Holy Spirit . . . will teach you all things . . . [and] will guide you into all truth' (John 14:26 and 16:13, NIV). He indeed is our first concordance for studying the Bible so that we may agree with its author's meaning! But, more profoundly, there really are four concordances:

1) Agreement or the concordance of the Holy Spirit, as we have mentioned above. We must always, as we sit before an open Bible, ask for the Holy Spirit to show us truth. We should expect and have faith that he will do that for which Jesus says he came.

2) However, the Holy Spirit uses other people and their work to interpret the Bible to us. In Acts 8:26-33, the Spirit sends Philip to interpret Isaiah 53:7-8 to the Ethiopian official. When we use a Bible concordance, it is like using someone else's work to unearth precious truths, but it is still the Holy Spirit's task to minister truth.

3) When we use a concordance, we are able to interpret a word or truth in agreement with the rest of the Bible. This is so that we don't contradict other truths, for truth must be in concordance or agreement with itself. This coherence is a necessary condition of something being true.

4) Finally, a concordance will help us to find Jesus in 'all the Scriptures', as Luke 24:27 says. Jesus promised that the Bible verses all pointed or witnessed to him (cf. John 5:39). By comparing Scripture with Scripture, we will see how Jesus must have extracted truth from the Bible. Paul seems to be teaching this in 1 Corinthians 2:12-13, when

he says that we have received the Spirit of God that we might know the things of God, and continues: 'we speak, not in words taught us by human wisdom but those taught by the Spirit, expressing [or comparing] spiritual truths in spiritual words.' This is so that we might have 'the mind of Christ' (verse 16).

A concordance is fantastically helpful. One wonders how Paul managed without one! Perhaps he knew the Scriptures so well he was one!

So concordance, and in particular *a* concordance, is one of the most important tools for studying the Bible.

By using a concordance, I saw that 'Bethel' (House of God) occurred for the first time in Scripture in Genesis 28:10-22 with Jacob's ladder, and so understood far more deeply what Jesus meant by using the Jacob (which means guile) story in John 1:47-51. 'You shall see heaven open and the angels of god ascending and descending on the Son of Man' (verse 51). So that's what the church is all about, I thought.

In Isaiah 53:4 the word used for stricken is that for someone being struck with leprosy. No wonder some Rabbis called Isaiah's 'Servant' the 'leprous' messiah. What a dramatic description of our Lord's work in bearing sin!

Isaiah 24 - 27 sprang to life when I saw, through a concordance that the 'Day of the LORD' comes seven times, revealing the content of that coming Messianic age.

I wondered why Jesus used two verbs which are synonymous for love in John 21:15-17? Then I used the concordance and found that the latter verb *phileo* meant 'friendship love', as in John 15:14, whereas the noun *philos* is translated 'friend'. 'Simon, are you really my friend?' Peter was hurt and now knew he did love Jesus!

Traditional concordances, such as *Strong's* and *Young's*, are based on the Authorized Version of the Bible. They are

IT CHANGED MY WORLD:

'It is only through this deeper understanding of God's Word that we can more fully understand our Father's will for us.' **Simon**

DEEPER

'exhaustive', not for us, but for those who aimed at putting every occurrence of a word in their work. These can be used, through the AV, with another version fairly easily, but are particularly helpful since they show the original words in Hebrew, Aramaic and Greek. Other versions, including the NIV, have also produced exhaustive concordances. IVP's *Bible Dictionary* is very helpful too - and of course the Internet has many resources in this area.

So go out, not just to buy coloured pens, but get hold of an exhaustive concordance. It will do you nothing but good. Mind you, I still use coloured pens too.

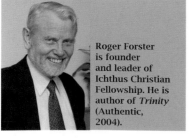

Roger Forster is founder and leader of Ichthus Christian Fellowship. He is author of *Trinity* (Authentic, 2004).

Greg Haslam

SPOTLIGHT

Tell us about a time when God spoke to you vividly and personally through the Bible.

My whole Christian life of some forty-two years now has been punctuated with many vivid occasions, but perhaps the most significant was in the third year of my ministry when I was desperate about the state of the church I was pastoring. The letter to the Laodicean church in Revelation 3 came alive to me in a remarkable way. I was gripped by its message and knew that in preaching from it our church would never be the same again. I called the message 'The Church that made Jesus sick!' and truly it was a watershed Sunday and the beginning of an amazing venture of renewal and change as Christ spoke prophetically into our situation. The church was transformed!

In recent years what has helped to keep the Bible fresh for you?

The discovery of the Bible's prophetic power to address my own life, as well as the circumstances around me. I treat the Bible as wholly inspired, completely infallible, and quite literally God's Word to man. This has shaped my concept of preaching, and the reverence and weight I accord to the Bible. This high view of Scripture predisposes us to see it as God's living word and therefore perennially fresh. This has been my experience for decades and is at the heart of my Christian life and ministry.

What does your regular practice of Bible reading look like?

I try to read the Bible through in one year, but often end up spending too long on specific books that grab me. Last year however, I worked through the new approach from CWR: *Cover to Cover Complete: Through the Bible as it happened.* This was in a different and more contemporary translation than my familiar NIV, and was marked by striking, yet succinct, meditations on the Scriptures. Something else that helps me is using accessible Bible commentaries that work through whole books, such as IVP's *The Bible Speaks Today,*

The Tyndale Old/New Testament Commentaries and volumes from *Preaching the Word* series edited by Kent Hughes. I have also used Tom Wright's new series of commentaries on the whole of the New Testament (published by SPCK) – brilliant!

What would you say to a Christian who is struggling to read the Bible?

This is a bit like responding to someone who is struggling to eat. You will surely starve, become sickly and even begin to 'die' if you neglect the Bible. I would recommend that if you are not already exposed to this essential benefit, then become part of a church where the Bible is handled well in weekly preaching and teaching. This will awaken an appetite to know more. In addition, I would recommend that you begin by reading the four gospels in slow, deliberate and meditative ways, and discover how Christ leaps from the page into your life. I'd also recommend a daily reading plan that takes you through the whole of the Bible and methodically develop the discipline to do this. It's likely to change your life! In addition, expose yourself to some of the best aids available: I recommend *Unlocking the Bible* by David Pawson (Collins).

What is your prayer for the Biblefresh initiative?

My fondest hope is that an increasingly biblically illiterate Church, which in many cases has removed itself from seriously handling the Bible, will once again bring the Scriptures back to centre stage in its preaching ministry, corporate life, and in each member's personal devotions and study of God's book. The results could be incalculable for our churches and nation.

Greg Haslam is Senior Minister at Westminster Chapel. He is author of *A Radical Encounter with God* (New Wine, 2008).

DAVID INSTONE-BREWER

TOXIC BIBLE

The Bible contains many regulations we'd prefer weren't there. Out-of-control teenagers should be stoned; a childless widow should have a son by her brother-in-law; people conquered in war should be enslaved; and even a fellow Jew who is unable to repay a debt should be enslaved (Deuteronomy 21:20–21; 25:5; 20:11; Leviticus 25:39–40).

When we read the Bible, we are looking over the shoulders of people living a few thousand years ago, for whom it was originally written. The Law of Moses was revolutionary to them, because it challenged them to live different lives. It didn't immediately transform them into a fully egalitarian society with a social benefit system and legally protected human rights, but it did point them in that direction, and pushed them as far as possible.

We can see what Israel would have been like without God's law, by examining the laws of surrounding nations at the time. For example, if a man died without a son, his widow had to produce an heir by sleeping with someone from her husband's family. This could be anyone ranging from her husband's grandfather to his young nephew. But the Law of Moses was more humane: the man had to be roughly her age (i.e. her husband's brother), and it was not compulsory.

Israelite rules of engagement in warfare were generous, according to opinion at the time (1 Kings 20:30). What we call genocide was the accepted destruction of populations who would feel obligated to avenge their fallen fathers by starting war again a few years later. Unlike other nations, Israel restricted this policy to enemies within their territory – when they conquered cities outside Israel, they killed only those individuals who actually attacked them Deuteronomy 20:10-17). There were no facilities for prisoner-of-war camps to enable more humane solutions. The Law of Moses discouraged warfare by banning pillage, which in other nations was the main way to pay soldiers. Israel was told that all plunder had to be 'devoted to the Lord' – destroyed (Joshua 6:18-19). This meant that Israel had only one motive for warfare: self-defence.

Penalties for crime in ancient Israel were harsher than we are comfortable with, but a death penalty is understandable when there are no secure prisons, especially while Israel lived in tents. Voluntary slavery is also understandable when banks didn't exist, because there was no way to pay a debt except by making a limited-term contract to work without wages. And while surrounding nations treated slaves as property without any human rights, the Law of Moses held a master responsible for any injury inflicted on a slave.

The penalty for theft was surprisingly mild in Israel – merely a return of the goods plus a fine – but in the surrounding nations, a thief who dug a hole through the mud wall of your house was executed and used as stuffing to fill in the hole. By contrast, surrounding nations merely prescribed a fine for injuring a low-born person, though if you injured one of the nobility you were punished with an 'eye for an eye'. The Law of Moses applied 'eye for an eye' to everyone i.e. it worked with the principle that everyone should be treated like nobility. The message was clear – all people should be treated as equal, and people are far more important than things, which was the opposite of the legal philosophy in other nations at the time.

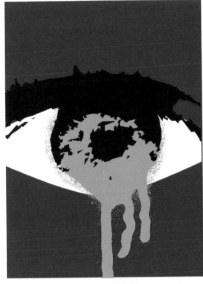

death penalty for less serious crimes, and although they still permitted slavery, they demanded that slaves should be treated almost like family members. They still regarded women as legally inferior, though they allowed them to own property and carry out business.

Jesus and the early Christians pushed things still further. Jesus taught that even Gentiles, lepers and prostitutes were loved by God – and demonstrated this personally. He allowed women to accompany his disciples and he encouraged them to learn – something done by no other ancient rabbi. Paul, contrary to normal custom, allowed women to attend his teaching sessions, though for the sake of public decency he told them not to take part by asking questions (1 Corinthians 14:34–35). The New Testament regarded women, slaves and non-slaves as equal (Galatians 3:28), and yet Christian women and slaves were told to be submissive to husbands and masters. The solution to this contradiction is seen when they explain the motive: they wanted to show that Christian women lived demure and moral lives, in order to encourage non-believers to examine the Gospel more carefully (1 Timothy 6:1–2; 1 Peter 3:1).

God's laws in the Bible constantly pushed humanity forward, as far as they could be pushed at the time. This means that the details of God's laws changed with society and circumstances, but the underlying message remained constant: the most valuable things on earth are not commodities but people. God loves and values people, and his law teaches us to do the same.

The Law of Moses may have been good for them, but does it do any good for us today? Its value lies in its message, which is eternal. Through these laws, God taught that people – all people – were supremely valuable. When you harvested your field, it was compulsory to leave something for the hungry poor. If you injured anyone, you were liable for severe punishment, even if that person was a slave or an unborn baby (Exodus 21:20–23).

By the time Jesus came, the Jews had taken on board some of these principles. They no longer wished to carry out the

David Instone-Brewer is Senior Research Fellow in Rabbinics and the New Testament at Tyndale House, Cambridge. He is author of *Traditions of the Rabbis* (Eerdmans, 2005).

TYNDALE HOUSE
RESIDENTIAL CENTRE
FOR BIBLICAL RESEARCH

story will not bother the Anglo-Saxons at all. They know all about Domesday, and they are glad to get more information about it! However, they will be shocked at the second story. Disloyalty and betrayal at Peter's level must never be forgiven, in their view. He doesn't deserve to live, let alone become the foremost disciple. They will be so appalled by this that they will want to throw the Bible down and read no more of it.

Of course, we think of the Anglo-Saxons as primitive, but someday others will think of us and our culture's dominant views as primitive. How can we use our time's standard of 'progressive' as the plumbline by which we decide which parts of the Bible are valid and which are not? Many of the beliefs of our grandparents and great-grandparents now seem silly and even embarrassing to us. That process is not going to stop now. Our grandchildren will find many of our views outmoded as well. Wouldn't it be tragic if we threw the Bible away over a belief that will soon look pretty weak or wrong? To stay away from Christianity because part of the Bible's teaching is offensive to you assumes that if there is a God he wouldn't have any views that upset you. Does that belief make sense?

I have one more bit of advice to people struggling with some of the Bible's teaching. We should make sure we distinguish between the major themes and message of the Bible and its less primary teachings. The Bible talks about the person and work of Christ and also about how widows should be regarded in the church. The first of these subjects is much more foundational. Without it the secondary teachings don't make sense. We should therefore consider the Bible's teachings in their proper order.

Let's take a hot issue today as a good example. If you say, 'I can't accept what the Bible says about gender roles,' you must keep in mind that Christians themselves differ over what some texts mean, as they do about many, many other things. However, they all confess in the words of the Apostles' Creed that Jesus rose from the dead on the third day. Don't worry about gender roles until you figure out what you think about the central teachings of the faith.

You may appeal, 'But I can't accept the Bible if what it says about gender is outmoded.' I would respond to that with this question - are you saying that because you don't like what the Bible says about sex that Jesus couldn't have been raised from the dead? I'm sure you wouldn't insist on such a non sequitur. If Jesus is the Son of God, then we have to take his teaching seriously, including his confidence in the authority of the whole Bible. If he is not who he says he is, why should we care what the Bible says about anything else?

Think of it like this. If you dive into the shallow end of the biblical pool, where there are many controversies over interpretation, you may get scraped up. But if you dive into the centre of the biblical pool, where there is consensus –

about the deity of Christ, his death and resurrection - you will be safe. It is therefore important to consider the Bible's core claims about who Jesus is and whether he rose from the dead before you reject it for its less central and more controversial teachings.

A trustworthy Bible or a Stepford God?

If we let our unexamined beliefs undermine our confidence in the Bible, the cost may be greater than we think. If you don't trust the Bible enough to let it challenge and correct your thinking, how could you ever have a personal relationship with God? In any truly personal relationship, the other person has to be able to contradict you. For example, if a wife is not allowed to contradict her husband, they won't have an intimate relationship. Remember the (two!) movies *The Stepford Wives*? The husbands of Stepford, Connecticut, decide to have their wives turned into robots who never cross the wills of their husbands. A Stepford wife was wonderfully compliant and beautiful, but no one would describe such a marriage as intimate or personal.

Now, what happens if you eliminate anything from the Bible that offends your sensibility and crosses your will? If you pick and choose what you want to believe and reject the rest, how will you ever have a God who can contradict you? You won't! You'll have a Stepford God! A God, essentially, of your own making, and not a God with whom you can have a relationship and genuine interaction. Only if your God can say things that outrage you and make you struggle (as in a real friendship or marriage!) will you know that you have got hold of a real God and not a figment of your imagination. So an authoritative Bible is not the enemy of a personal relationship with God. It is the precondition for it.

Tim Keller is the founding pastor of Redeemer Presbyterian Church in New York.

Taken from *The Reason for God* by Tim Keller (Hodder & Stoughton, 2009). Used by permission.

David Wilkinson

Tell us about a time when God spoke to you vividly and personally through the Bible.

One of the times when God has spoken most vividly and personally was as a research student when my work was in the origin of galaxies and the universe. One day I was reading Colossians 1:15–20 and was caught by the verse which states that all things cohere in Christ. It struck me in a brand new way that the reason I was able to do science, the reason that there are laws of physics at the heart of the universe, is because all creation has coherence and, further than that, Jesus is the source of that coherence. Therefore to do science is to explore the coherence put at the heart of the universe, whose source is Jesus. To do science is a Christian ministry.

In recent years what has helped to keep the Bible fresh for you?

The Bible is continually fresh for me if I allow it to speak to me. Allowing it to speak to me means that I often change the method of reading and study. I have grown to appreciate the Anglican cycle of Morning Prayer here in St John's, Durham University, which reads whole passages of Scripture every morning. I like Bible commentaries, I like the opportunity of preaching from Scripture and I like reading the Bible now on my mobile phone. Perhaps most of all, the thing that's kept the Bible fresh for me is reading the Bible together with colleagues and fellow church members and seeing God speak within the sense of group study.

What does your regular practice of Bible reading look like?

My regular practice of Bible reading at the moment is about reading through the Bible in one year, using a rather old outline of how one does that, but reading the text directly from my mobile phone. I am not a good morning person so I have never been one who has been able to get up very early in the morning, but I do make time during the day, sometimes at lunchtime, sometimes just after breakfast to read the Bible then.

What would you say to a Christian who is struggling to read the Bible?

Sometimes it does require discipline and sometimes you just have to persevere, but there are a huge number of ways to read the Bible. It is good to read it alone but also with others. An amazing thing about the Bible is that as you persevere, so it will shape, transform and excite you.

What is your prayer for the Biblefresh initiative?

That people would simply be excited with the gift of the Scriptures, the gift of God's own Word in a way that's accessible to us every day. But further, my prayer would be that we learn to understand and live Scripture, rather than just knowing about it.

David Wilkinson is Principal of St John's College, Durham. He is editor of *The Call and the Commission* (Paternoster, 2008).

THE CALL AND THE COMMISSION

To do science is to explore the coherence put at the heart of the universe, whose source is Jesus.

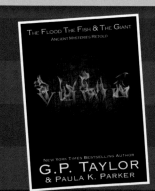

FRESHEN UP

BIBLE TRAINING IDEAS

KIM WALKER

Been inspired by reading about how the Bible has impacted ordinary people's lives?

Fascinated by the amazing stories contained in the Bible?

Want to delve into the Bible for some more treasure?

DON'T JUST THINK ABOUT IT: DO SOMETHING!

What not try a Bible studies course? There are lots of courses on offer all over the UK and many do not require any previous theological qualifications. There's something to suit everyone: full-time, part-time, distance learning, online, evening and one-off weekend courses.

Or how about booking a place at a Christian festival? Festivals give you the opportunity to meet up with like-minded Christians, join with them to worship, hear from great speakers, be challenged and have fun together. During 2011 many festivals will focus on the Bible or run special Biblefresh seminars, to equip you to go deeper into God's Word. Why not organize a group visit from your church?

DON'T KNOW HOW TO GET STARTED?

We have lots of suggestions of Bible colleges and Christian festivals for you to try on the next few pages, so why not take action and book your place now?

Kim Walker is Senior Information Officer at the Evangelical Alliance.

MY FAVOURITE BIBLE VERSE

FIONA CASTLE
SPEAKER AND AUTHOR

'I am praying not only for these disciples but also for all who will ever believe in me because of their message.' (John 17:20, NLT)

I find it amazing and wonderful that in this verse Jesus was praying for me! It is only because of the faithfulness of the disciples that the message has been passed down the generations for 2,000 years, and the onus now is on me to ensure that those of my generation and the ones to follow will be part of that same prayer.

If**you****want**to...

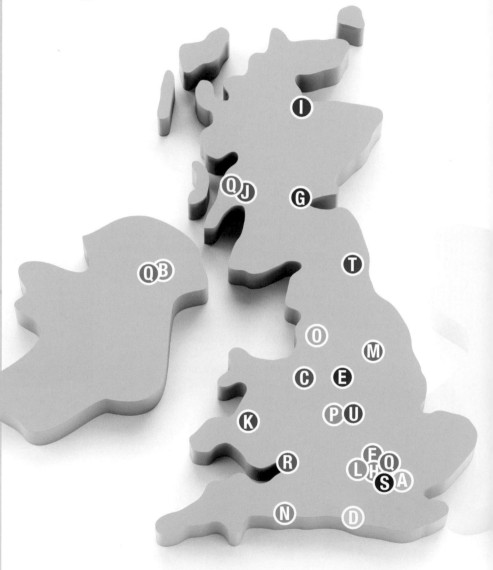

...deepen your understanding of the Bible, there are a number of colleges that offer short courses, part time courses or longer distance learning courses. Here are some suggestions.

A Allnations
www.allnations.ac.uk

B Belfast Bible College
www.belfastbiblecollege.com

C Birmingham Christian College
www.bhxc.ac.uk

D Christ for the Nations
www.christforthenationsuk.org

E Cliff College
www.cliffcollege.ac.uk

F European Training Programme
www.eurotp.org

G Faith Mission Bible College
www.faithmission.org/college/college.htm

H Global Action
www.global-act.org.uk/glomos_london

I Highland Theological College
www.htc.uhi.ac.uk/course.htm

J International Christian College
www.icc.ac.uk

K Kings Evangelical Divinity School
www.midbible.ac.uk

L London School of Theology
www.lst.ac.uk

M Mattersey Hall
www.matterseyhall.co.uk

N Moorlands
www.moorlands.ac.uk/courses_elivate.htm

O Nazarene Theological College
www.nazarene.ac.uk

P New Testament Church of God
www.ntcg.org.uk/education

Q Proclamation Trust
Cornhill Training Course
www.proctrust.org.uk/cornhill/cornhill.htm

R Redcliffe College
www.redcliffe.org

S Spurgeon's
www.spurgeons.ac.uk

T St John's College, Durham
www.dur.ac.uk/st-johns.college/cranmer/

U St John's College, Nottingham
www.stjohns-nottm.ac.uk

FESTIVALS

If**you**want**to**...

...increase your Bible knowledge, there are festivals throughout the year that give you an opportunity to be refreshed in your learning. There are dozens of these – big and small – so here is a selection.

A Children's Ministry
January, Eastbourne

B Clan Gathering
July, St Andrew's

C Cliff College Festival
May, Derbyshire

D Christian Resources Exhibition
May, Surrey

E Detling
August, Kent

F ECG
April, Llandudno

G Keswick
July, Cumbria

H Leading Edge
August, Warwick

I New Horizon
July, Coleraine

J New Wine
July & August, Somerset and Nottinghamshire

K New Wine Cymru
August, Builth Wells

L New Word Alive
April, Pwllheli

M Momentum
August, Somerset

N Pentecost
May, London

O Roots
April-May, Southport

P Salt & Light
February, Oxford

Q Soul Survivor
July & August, Somerset

R Summer Fire
July, Southport

S Summer Madness
July, Belfast

T Spring Harvest
April, Lincolnshire and Somerset

U Worldwide
August, Bangor, Northern Ireland

V Youthwork
November, Eastbourne

TRANSLATING THE MESSAGE

BIBLE TRANSLATION

NICK SPENCER

WORD ON THE STREET

According to research commissioned by the public theology think tank Theos, 12 per cent of Britons read the Bible once a week or more. The figure may surprise and encourage. It is, after all, somewhat higher than the proportion that attends church that frequently. More disturbing, if less surprising, is the statistic that 61 per cent of people never read the Bible at all.

Just as more people consider themselves Christians than ever darken a church door, however, so the public's attitude to the Bible is more positive than their reading habits would suggest. According to the same survey, 26 per cent of people agree that the Bible is 'the divinely inspired Word of God', 37 per cent say it is 'a useful book of guidance and advice for our lives (but not the Word of God)', and 19 per cent call it 'beautiful literature but otherwise irrelevant for us today'. Only 11 per cent say they think it is 'an irrelevant and

dangerous collection of ancient myths'.

We are familiar with this 'cognitive dissonance'. We may not be a Christian country in the way that we were a century ago, but that does not mean we are not a Christian country. Many people have an imprecise and hesitant affinity with Christianity and even with the Bible, an affinity that is not hindered by ignorance of both.

However, this is no excuse for complacency. Younger people are less likely to read the Bible (71 per cent of 18-

IT CHANGED MY WORLD:

'When studying God's Word the times are precious. The encounters are second to none. Just to be in his Word and in his presence is the best thing ever.' **Fran**

PRECIOUS

24s never do vs. 45 per cent of over 65s), and they are also more likely to be hostile to it (19 per cent of 18-24s deem it 'irrelevant and dangerous' compared with 6 per cent of over 65s).

It is too early to tell whether these differences are because of (what researchers call) the 'age effect', whereby people's opinions are determined by how old they are and, thus, change with age (political affiliation is a classic example of this); or whether it is the 'cohort effect', whereby opinions are determined by the generation to which people belong and don't change (significantly) with age (e.g. 'Baby Boomer' opinions).

There is good reason to believe that people's attitudes to the Bible are determined by the cohort effect, and as Generation Ys age, they will retain much of the scriptural scepticism. If so, this presents a real challenge for the Bible in twenty-first-century Britain.

What, therefore, can we do?

There is of course no simple solution to this (except possibly national revival, although social research tends not to rely on such things), but we might learn something from the broader social context in which these trends are occurring.

Just as falling church attendance has occurred and needs to be understood alongside falling membership levels for other comparable organizations, such as political parties and trade unions, so the public's engagement with the Bible needs to be read alongside two particular contemporary social trends.

The first is the move away from the written word towards the visual (and malleable) image. We are a less literary society today than of recent decades. We read the Bible less because we read less.

The second is the steep decline in trust that has affected almost every public institution over the last thirty years. There is a serious anti-institutional streak in modern British society. Authority and institutions are in tension with the liberty and individualism we so treasure and they suffer for it.

Given these two trends, an authoritative book was always likely to struggle in our society.

However, there may be good news. Dislike reading and authority as we do, we do like a bit of entertainment. And whatever else people say about the Bible, even its fiercest critics recognize that it is a very entertaining book. In the words of the novelist Sebastian Faulks (neither one of the Bible's fiercest critics nor one of its most fanatical advocates), 'of the 100 greatest stories ever told, 99 are probably in the Old Testament and the other is in Homer'.

Promoting the Bible for its entertainment value would have scandalized previous generations of evangelicals. But if Paul was prepared to become a Jew for the Jews and weak for the weak . . .

Nick Spencer is Director of Studies at Theos. He is author of *Darwin and God* (SPCK, 2009).

Theos
The public theology think tank

LUKE WALTON

THE APPLE OF MY EYE

I think I will have this article in the handbook by the *skin of my teeth*. *The writing has been on the wall* for some time that I would leave this until the last moment, unlike those, *the salt of the earth*, who always prove themselves to be dependable.

The availability of God's words in the English language for the first time had a revolutionary impact on our culture. So deep and lasting has it been, that it is quoted every day by billions of people who do not even realize what they are doing. It is still quoted deliberately by statesmen and presidents and peacemakers and carers; it has and continues to inspire a remarkable range of responses.

Throughout history, from Doctor Barnardo to Martin Luther King, the Bible has stirred social consciences and encouraged people to work for a better world. In his book *12 Books that Changed the World*, Melvyn Bragg included the King James Version of the Bible because, he argues, hearing God's words in the English language was key to the development of democracy first in the UK and then in the US.

Many of the world's famous charities and social causes also owe their origins to people who were inspired by the Bible. Even the English word 'charity' comes from the Bible. It's a translation of the *caritas* (love), which was used in the Latin Vulgate.

The Bible says that Jesus told his followers to heal the sick and to teach all nations (Matthew 10:8; 28:19,20). So it's perhaps not surprising that by drawing on the Bible, Christians have made real strides in the fields of healthcare and education. Both the birth of the hospital and the hospice movement came from the inspiration of Scripture, as did professional nursing.

Quintin Hogg (1845-1903) felt moved by God to educate the urchins who roamed the streets of London. Pupils at his 'ragged school' learned to read through studying the Bible. Hogg later went on to establish the first polytechnic, with Bible classes as a core part of the curriculum.

Yet if charitable work is not a surprising response to Scripture, the impact on some of the arts world is. We might realize that the Bible has been a rich source of inspiration for musicians when we hear, for instance, Handel's Messiah playing every Christmas and Easter. Likewise we know that great galleries are lined with the intriguing characters of the Bible, brought to life by many famous painters and sculptors.

But the Bible has reached further and deeper into our culture than that. Its stories have been brought to life in epic productions of stage and screen. Biblical descriptions of religious architecture have inspired the construction of many beautiful churches and cathedrals. The Bible has also personally influenced some of the leading lights of the theatre and the motion picture industry.

For example J. Arthur Rank (1888-1972) has been hailed as the saviour of the British film industry. But he was also a man who lived by faith.

Rank started out in the family flour business, but felt called by God to switch his attention to the movies. 'I am in films because of the Holy Spirit,' he later said.

Early on, he realized the role that well-made films could have in promoting the gospel. In 1933, he got involved in the Religious Film Society and began bankrolling the production of religious films, moving into the industry to revive the British industry and to challenge the world domination of Hollywood.

Rank became a major force in British film, buying up movie theatres and film companies. At its peak, the Rank Organization, of which he was the chairman, owned the Odeon cinema chain, several film studios, a series of production companies and even a distribution arm. In 1934, he built the famous Pinewood Studios (where James Bond is filmed). The Rank Organization became a global organization and he gave many British directors and actors their lucky breaks.

Yet, Rank was not only a captain of industry. He was also a Sunday school teacher in the Methodist Church. And his Methodist faith was the driving force in his life. In a 1952 interview, Rank spoke about the importance of Romans 1:17

for him. He remarked: 'Faith; we all live by faith. All this [the Rank headquarters] is nothing but faith.'

This is just one example among many. In all spheres of life – politics, education, medicine, science and the arts – the Bible has shaped the development of the world as we know it, and continues to do so today.

Luke Walton is Arts Development Officer at the Bible Society.

In all spheres of life - politics, education, medicine, science and the arts - the Bible has shaped the development of the world as we know it.

THE APPLE OF MY EYE

MARTIN MANSER

SCAPEGOATS, SHAMBLES & SHIBBOLETHS

The Queen's English from the King James Bible

A selection of phrases from everyday life that originated in the King James Version of the Bible:

COVER A MULTITUDE OF SINS

And above all things have fervent charity among yourselves: for charity shall cover the multitude of sins.
1 Peter 4:8

It is shockingly easy to harbour grudges and allow resentment to take root, blossom and flourish - especially where we feel that we have been harshly treated by another person. When we believe ourselves to be the victim of some wrong or injustice, our resentment - not to mention our ability to quantify and classify each wound - builds. Peter's remedy for this festering cancer that can destroy both individuals and groups is love.

As the King James Version puts it, *charity shall cover the multitude of sins*. It neither ignores them nor pretends they don't exist. It knows they are real and it takes them seriously, but nevertheless chooses to cover them so they needn't be brought out into the open for all to see. Often the expression is heard in situations where something good is held to make up for whatever faults and mistakes there are and the latter are deliberately overlooked.

A DROP IN THE BUCKET/OCEAN

Behold, the nations are as a drop of a bucket, and are counted as the small dust of the balance: behold, he taketh up the isles as a very little thing.
Isaiah 40:15

A drop in the bucket is an insignificant quantity when compared with the contents of a bucket or the vastly larger ocean. So the idea being alluded to here is that of insignificance when set alongside something that is immeasurably greater. The verses could seem to imply that God shows contempt for the nations, but the real sense is that the nations are so small and insignificant compared with him that he is not intimidated by them in the slightest: he takes notice of them because he chooses to, not because they can force him to. The expression is frequently used to describe what happens when someone performs an apparently futile action that is perceived to have no impact upon a situation. In the context, Isaiah is explaining how from a divine perspective, even the mighty nations appear minute. They are rather like a speck of dust that has found its way onto a set of scales - unlikely to be seen and certainly failing to register any increase in weight. Or like the view of the world we get from a plane - tiny from our lofty perspective. God is incomparably greater than us.

EAT, DRINK AND BE MERRY, FOR TOMORROW WE DIE

And behold joy and gladness, slaying oxen, and killing sheep, eating flesh, and drinking wine: let us eat and drink; for tomorrow we shall die.

Isaiah 22:13

When we say, *let's eat, drink and be merry* – with or without its corollary, *for tomorrow we die,* the call is to enjoy ourselves while we can, because we don't know what the future may hold. It may come as a surprise to discover that this well known saying and its variations occur three times in the Bible. It seems to be advocating a life of hedonistic enjoyment: you may as well get what you can out of existence because sooner or later it is going to come to an end. The reality is that on two of these occurrences the viewpoint elicits disapproval: in Isaiah the city of Jerusalem is being condemned for its inappropriate behaviour, and when it is cited in Jesus' parable in Luke 12 the words are uttered by a man labelled as a rich fool. Only in Ecclesiastes 8 is the phrase tempered by the acknowledgement, in the last verse of the book, that God will ultimately judge everyone's conduct. In reality therefore, the self-indulgent outlook is not being encouraged, but condemned. It might be a valid philosophy in a meaningless world, but it has no place in the world the Bible describes.

THE ELEVENTH HOUR

And about the eleventh hour he went out, and found others standing idle, and saith unto them, Why stand ye here all the day idle?

Matthew 20:6

The *eleventh hour* is that point just before a deadline, when it is almost too late to change anything – but when the situation may just be susceptible to change. In the parable it was the last chance that potential workers had of being hired by the owner of the vineyard, which highlights the difference in references to time: this is not just before midnight, as we might take it to be, but the end of the working day. In Jesus' story, the eleventh hour is not the last chance to save the day but the door to a positive, perhaps unexpected, situation: these men get to do some work after all, and are paid for a full day despite only working for the last hour. In God's plan, good can come even at the eleventh hour.

My bone cleaveth to my skin and to my flesh, and I am escaped with the skin of my teeth.

FALL FROM GRACE

Christ is become of no effect unto you, whosoever of you are justified by the law; ye are fallen from grace.
Galatians 5:4

To *fall from grace* means to lose some high position, important post or special favour. Captains of industry, politicians and those in the public eye are frequently notable candidates for this dishonour. Very often their demise is rapid and associated with some scandal or indiscretion discovered by the media and tutted over by a disapproving audience – doubtless glad that their lives aren't subject to a similar scrutiny. Paul used the expression when speaking to the Galatians. He was deeply concerned that, having entered into the Christian faith through an understanding of God's gift of undeserved grace, the people were now trying to improve their standing by attempting to fulfil the old requirements of the Jewish legal system. Rather than seeing this as an upward step, giving an improvement in their standing, the apostle believed it to be a retrograde, downward fall.

OUT OF THE MOUTHS OF BABES

Out of the mouth of babes and sucklings hast thou ordained strength because of thine enemies, that thou mightest still the enemy and the avenger.
Psalm 8:2

When parents hear their child make some insightful remark, or perhaps express an opinion about a guest that they themselves would not have dared utter, he or she might laughingly be heard to say, *Out of the mouths of babes and infants . . .* What is meant is that a child, in his or her naivety, innocence, and possibly ignorance of social mores, has said something that older and supposedly wiser people have failed to observe – or have been too diplomatic to say themselves. The phrase appears in Psalm 8 where its inclusion highlights God's use of these apparently insignificant members of the human race to shame those who ought to know better.

SKIN OF MY TEETH

My bone cleaveth to my skin and to my flesh, and I am escaped with the skin of my teeth.
Job 19:20

Tooth enamel is the hardest substance in our bodies. That makes it good for biting. Skin is one of the softest parts of our bodies. That makes it good for grazing, cutting and peeling. If we had skin on our teeth, meals would be drawn out, chewy affairs – but we don't. When the writer of Job talks about the skin of his teeth, he means avoiding something by an incredibly small, perhaps imperceptible, amount. When we say we have *escaped something by the skin of our teeth,* we mean we have only just managed to steer clear of some disaster or tragedy.

THE STRAIGHT AND NARROW

Because strait is the gate, and narrow is the way, which leadeth unto life, and few there be that find it.
Matthew 7:14

The *straight and narrow* is a path that is considered to be good from a moral perspective. If someone strays from it they usually become the object of self-righteous reproach or, if they are in the limelight, the censure of the tabloid press. Jesus used the expression in the Sermon on the Mount to describe the little-trod pathway to heavenly blessing. He contrasted it with the much travelled wide or broad road that leads to destruction. The word straight here was originally *strait*, meaning 'narrow' (as in the Straits of Gibraltar), not actually straight: so there is a narrow gate that is therefore hard to find, and a narrow path that is uncomfortable and difficult to follow.

Taken from *Scapegoats, Shambles and Shibboleths* by Martin Manser (Hodder & Stoughton, 2009). Used by permission.

Martin Manser is a reference book editor, language trainer and consultant.

KWAME BEDIAKO

SCRIPTURE AS THE INTERPRETER OF CULTURE AND TRADITION

What is Culture?

Culture comprises far more than just music, dance, artefacts and the like. Our culture is our world view, that is, fundamental to our understanding of who we are, where we have come from and where we are going. It is everything in us and around us that defines us and shapes us. When we turn to Christ as Lord, we are turning over to him all that is in us, all that is about us and all that is around us that has defined and shaped us. Thus salvation encompasses not just our 'souls', but also our culture at its deepest level. We need to allow Scripture to become the interpreter of who we are in the specific concrete sense of who we are in our cultures and traditions.

What is Scripture?

But acknowledging the centrality of Scripture to our identity does not mean that we demonize our own traditional culture or learn to quote certain verses and chapters as proof texts to support particular positions we hold because of our denominational or traditional background. The centrality of Scripture is more fundamental and its significance much larger than that.

Scripture is a Prism

When light passes through a prism, a rainbow of colours is revealed. Similarly, when our cultures pass through the prism of Scripture, we see them in a new way. The light and shade intrinsic to our cultures are revealed. We are no longer being defined by our traditions, but are allowing Scripture to interpret those traditions.

Scripture is a Record of God's Engagement with Culture

Scripture is more than just a record of the history and religion of Israel and the early church. Rather, it records God's dealings with his people and with their culture, and is itself the fruit of that engagement. It thus provides a yardstick or a model for encouraging, identifying and controlling all subsequent engagements of gospel and culture in the continuing divine-human encounter that characterizes our faith.

Scripture is a Road Map

Scripture is the authoritative road map on our journey of faith, a journey that began before we first believed in Christ. This road map reminds us that the journey we are on did not begin at the point when we ourselves received the map. By looking at the map in Scripture, we can see where we have come from and how we got to where we are. It also points us in the direction we are to take if we are to reach our destination. This understanding is one that the early preachers of the gospel stressed when they so often used the phrase 'according to the Scriptures'. Paul reminds Timothy of the guiding role of Scripture (2 Timothy 3:16). He demonstrates its use when he recounts part of the history of the Israelites and concludes, 'These things happened to them as examples and were written down as warnings for us' (1 Corinthians 10:11).

Too often, preachers tend to pick a particular text and use it as a launch pad for presenting their own ideas, but apostolic preaching was not like that. It presented the meaning of Scripture as a whole and applied that meaning to the concrete cultural and social situation of the hearers. That is what we have to do if Scripture is to be the road map for getting us to our destination.

Scripture is our history

All the references to Scripture in the New Testament relate to the Old Testament, although the majority of those addressed would have been Gentiles, who did not share the Jews' cultural background. Yet, Paul refers to 'our forefathers' when speaking to Gentile Corinthians (1 Corinthians 10:1). Israel's history had become their 'adoptive' history, for all believers in Christ become children of Abraham (Galatians 3:26-29) and are grafted into the original olive tree (Romans 11:7-20). And all believers were slaves who have been set free (Galatians 4:7). All of us have been adopted into Christ, with our traditions, and are therefore transformed, with our traditions. The God of Israel is not a tribal God but the God who created all humanity.

Scripture is the Basis of our Identity

The earliest church was tempted to see Gentile Christians as second-class Jews, latecomers. But at the Council of Jerusalem (Acts 15) the apostles recognized that God was doing something new. Paul makes the same point when he writes as if there are now three categories of persons: Jews, Gentiles and something new, called the church of God (1 Corinthians 10:32; 2 Corinthians 5:17; Ephesians 2:14-18).

In the early decades of the church, some Christian writers spoke of Christians as a third race. The first race was the Jews; the second, the Gentiles; and the third was the Christians. The basis of this new identity was religious, not ethnic, national, social or cultural in the narrow sense. We have become 'a kingdom of priests to serve God' (Revelation 1:5-6; 1 Peter 2:9-10).

Scripture is our Story

Scripture is not just a holy book from which we extract teaching and biblical principles. Rather, it is a story in which we participate. When David Livingstone preached in Africa in the nineteenth century, he is said to have always referred to the Bible as the 'message from the God whom you know'. In other words, Scripture speaks to us because Scripture speaks about us. And it speaks about us because we are a part of the gospel we preach. Paul was very aware of this. He emphasized that God had had mercy on him, and now he was called to preach to others (1 Corinthians 15:8-11).

Africans have a strong sense of their pre-Christian religious journey and should be alive to this participation in Scripture. This was certainly true of the Liberian prophet William Wadé Harris (1865-1929). He was the first distinctive African Christian prophet of modern times, and a man who brought many people into the church. Harris cut himself off from his Grebo life and family in a radical conversion, but he did not live without ancestors or a community. He simply changed his family connections to those based on faith in Christ as known through the Scriptures. His was a spirituality of vital participation totally indigenous to his African way of being within a community. He did not think in terms of what Moses saw or Jesus did in the Bible, but of how his new ancestors, Moses, Elijah, and supremely Jesus Christ, interacted with him. That was how he broke through to many people and they became Christians.

In African culture, participation in a common life constitutes community and marks out an ethnic group. When a libation is poured, the community recites the names of all those who are absent, treating them as present. Traditional believers summon their ancestors, and they believe that these ancestors are present at the ceremony that follows. (Do we have a similar confidence that Jesus is present when we pray?)

Scripture is not just a holy book from which we extract teaching and biblical principles. Rather, it is a story in which we participate.

PARTICIPATE

In Christian terms, we participate in Christ, and thus also in the resources and powers of the entire community composed of those who are also one with Christ through the Spirit. This community includes both the living and the dead (Luke 20:33–38). It is a transcendent community in which the human components experience and share in the divine life and nature (2 Peter 1:4).

Bringing Scripture and Culture Together

We should not focus on extracting principles from the Bible and applying these to culture. Scripture is not a book existing independently of us. Scripture is the living testimony to what God has done and continues to do, and we are part of that testimony. The characters in Scripture are both our contemporaries and our ancestors. Their triumphs and failures help us understand our own journey of faith (Romans 11:18).

Scripture is not something we only believe in, it is something we share in. This is why the people in the Bible will not be made perfect without us (Hebrews 11:40), nor we without them. The application of Scripture to our cultures is a gradual process of coming together, of life touching life. Our particular culture encounters the activity of God in building up a community of his people throughout history, a community that now includes us and our particular traditions, history and culture. We will gradually come to share in a family likeness that is not measured by ethnic particularity but by nothing less than Christ himself (Ephesians 4:13).

Scripture and culture are like merging circles, gradually coming to have one centre as we increasingly recognize ourselves in Scripture and Scripture becomes more and more recognizable as our story.

The process of bringing the gospel and culture together takes more than one generation. To look for a once and for all biblical 'answer' to a particular cultural problem is to misunderstand the process whereby a community and people come to see themselves as called into the people of God and come to participate in that community.

The process takes several generations, both ancient and modern. All the endeavours of believers from many backgrounds wrestling with gospel and culture are an integral part of our story. To fully understand the impact of the gospel engaging with any particular cultural environment we need to know of the struggle of ancient Israel to come to terms with the uniqueness and the majesty of Yahweh, their backslidings, apostasy, calamity, tragedy and triumphs. We also need to know how African earth shrines relate to God's way. We need to know how the gospel was brought from Alexandria to Axum, how it was taken from Ireland to the English, how it was taken from south-eastern Ghana to the Upper East Region. No part of the story of the people of God is alien to any other part of the story or is more important than any other part. The gospel has no permanent resident culture. It is as we take the experiences and the struggle in one context and funnel them through our own reading and experience of the Scriptures in our mother tongue that we find that other Christian stories illuminate our story.

Scripture, Language and Culture

Mother-tongue Scripture has a fundamental place in the engagement of gospel and culture. If people recognize that Onyankopon (as God is called by the Akan of Ghana), the God they have known from time immemorial, is their Saviour, and that the coming of the gospel is what they have looked forward to, then God is continuing to ensure that they will hear him each in their own language so that they can marvel at his majesty and his love for them. Our mother tongue is the language in which God speaks to each of us. He does not speak in a sacred language, but in ordinary language, so that we may hear him and realize that this gospel is about us and that we have been invited to join a company drawn from every people, tribe, tongue, nation and language (Revelation 7:9).

Kwame Bediako (1945–2008) was the founding rector of the Akrofi-Christaller Institute for Theology, Mission, and Culture, in Ghana.

Taken from *Africa Bible Commentary* ed. by Tokunboh Adeyemo (Zondervan, 2006) Used by permission.

KRISH KANDIAH

PRIMARY TEXTS: HELPING KIDS WITH THE BIBLE

My 10-year-old son can name any episode of *The Simpsons* from the title sequence sofa scene alone. My 9-year-old son can quote large chunks of dialogue from his favourite *Simpsons* episodes. My 8-year-old daughter can tell you a *Simpsons* character beginning with each letter of the alphabet. My 3-year-old daughter can sing *The Simpsons* theme tune. And between all of us we know a frightening amount of trivia about the Springfield community from the tragic story of Frank Grimes, to the secret life of Principal Skinner, to the Simpsons's extended family tree.

All this from twenty minutes of family time after tea, five nights a week, and it begs the questions: What would happen to this generation if the Bible Story was grasped as convincingly? What if it was the Bible's implicit values that were being absorbed as regularly? What if it was God's words that were being etched on their minds at this young age?

There is a tension here, and it is not only a question of TV or family devotions after tea. For those of us who were force-fed the Bible growing up, we fear pushing our children away from God, and play down the amount of Bible we offer our kids. For those of us who came to faith later in life we are keen to get as much of the Bible into them so they can grow up nourished with the wisdom of God's Word in their hearts. How can we walk the middle line to help our children to develop a taste and an appetite for Scripture? Or to use a different metaphor, how can we help our kids to discover the treasures of the Bible and appreciate its value?

The following suggestions are a variety of ways we can help our kids encounter God's Word that hope to be both informative and inspirational. During this Biblefresh year, you may want to try some of them out.

It's never too early to introduce your children to God. It is good for them to hear you speaking to God, even if it is for patience in the middle of the night! And when they are learning their first words, a simple prayer like, 'Dear God, thank you, amen' will ensure that relating to God predates their earliest memories. There is a host of really good Bible resources for toddlers from DVDs such as *VeggieTales* to CDs that everyone will enjoy singing along to on long car journeys, to a wealth of board books and 'first' Bibles.

Bedtime is an important bonding time with kids and parents, but also between kids, parents and God. Because I am often at work most of the day, I try whenever possible to come home and take responsibility for taking time to talk and listen with each of my children as they settle down at the end of the day. Whether we are talking over the dilemmas of the day, or reading a school book, or tidying up Lego, there always seems to be a wealth of opportunity to talk about faith, God

eyes, and heard them through a child's ears. (For a long time, one of my kids thought I was talking about the Weirdo of Zarephath!)

Remembering to thank God for the meal when we sit down to eat as a family has often inspired interesting discussions about global justice. Recalling stories read during the day such as *The Gruffalo* has inspired philosophical chats about stories that are fictional, and stories that are real – like the Bible. Talking about what is going on at school often raises ethical dilemmas to discuss. These conversations can be just as valuable as structured devotionals as we model how our beliefs impact our decisions, our worldviews and our behaviour.

Walking as a family is also a prime opportunity for spiritual input. Whether it is pointing out the intricacies of God's creation, or playing multiple-choice Q&A games based on Bible stories, or posing moral dilemmas, or coming across people or animals we can help, we find that we can incorporate a sense of fun and family bonding into the serious business of passing on God's Word to our children.

Finally, watching TV and films together is another useful and natural connection point between us, our kids and God. It does mean that I have to sit and watch with them, rather than work on my laptop or go off and make the tea, but that is no real hardship for me! Some of the best God-conversations we have had as a family is when we pause halfway through a show for dinner and discuss the quandaries and conflicts and themes. We try to guess what is going to happen next, work out why the characters have got into such a mess, or discuss what we would do in a similar situation. This allows us not to accept unconsciously all the values of a movie, but to engage consciously with the movie – both the good and bad points. Sometimes there's opportunity to talk about how movies are echoes of biblical stories like *Finding Nemo* (Prodigal Son), *Shrek* (Judges), *Superman* (Incarnation). Sometimes the discussions are more about biblical values such as responsibility and respect for other people – usually after *The Simpsons* . . .

and daily life. We also experiment with a variety of material to take it one step further. Helping my children work through daily Bible reading notes, or reading biographies of great Christian leaders from the past such as *10 Boys Who Changed the World* or *10 Girls Who Made a Difference* (Irene Howat, Christian Focus), or memorizing parts of the psalms have all been helpful to mix things up a bit, as well as sharing prayer requests or taking it in turns to thank God for one thing each.

Sometimes bedtime simply doesn't work as spiritual time. My kids seem to go through phases where they are too tired to get their words out right, let alone remember anything we are reading. We should pick up on these cues and make an effort then to weave the Bible into the rest of the day. In Deuteronomy God tells his people to place Scriptures on their doorposts and on the sleeves of their garments so that they talk about God wherever they go. This is a fantastic model of not restricting God's influence to a ten-minute slot at the end of the day, but allowing God's Word to impact our everyday life.

When my children were smaller, I used to bath them three at a time and I certainly had a captive audience! They were at the age where everything was brand new, and I loved watching their faces as I told them Bible stories. It was a learning experience for me too as I saw the stories through a child's

Krish Kandiah is Executive Director: Churches in Mission at the Evangelical Alliance and author of *Twenty-Four: Integrating Faith and Real Life* (Authentic, 2008).

DAVID BENDOR-SAMUEL

ACCESS FOR ALL

A man named Jimmy lies in hospital slowly dying. A friend called Bob comes to visit and offers Jimmy a Bible. Jimmy is an atheist and won't have anything to do with God or religion, even refusing discussion with his Christian son. However he takes the Bible and, even more surprisingly, he reads it. Three days before he dies he meets with God and accepts salvation.

Surely we shouldn't be surprised at the power of Scripture to transform a life, in fact, we should expect it. What makes this story noteworthy is Bob. Bob has a learning disability. If any other person had offered Jimmy the Bible he would have refused it. But from Bob he took it - why?

Bob had spent the first forty years of his life in an institution after being abandoned on a doorstep when only a few weeks old. Bob then moved to a house in the community where the manager was a Christian - Jimmy's son as it happens. Bob was invited to church where he discovered people who valued him. He also discovered, through others making Scripture accessible to him, that God valued him as well.

Bob, who once felt he himself had no value, offered Jimmy a gift that the giver treasured more than anything else in the world. How could Jimmy refuse? There are two miracles here: Jimmy ending up in heaven certainly, but in some ways the bigger miracle was that Bob, as a disabled person, was enabled to understand and value Scripture. The power of the Bible has to be unwrapped, its light revealed to show the way - and for far too many people with disabilities this does not happen.

Disabled people have to grapple with one or more of three challenges in accessing Scripture:

- physical access,
- access to information, and
- access to understanding.

Different disabilities throw up differing barriers. Physically handling a Bible is challenging for some. For others, a blind person for instance, the media used prevents the information within being accessed. For those with learning disabilities, understanding God's Word can be problematic.

Surely this is a marginal issue? Not so. There are an estimated 600 million disabled people globally. If they were a nation it would be the third largest in the world after China and India. In the UK the figure is around 9.5 million, or 16 per cent of the population. Bob is one among 1.5 million people in the UK with a learning disability. And it's not as though the world is divided neatly into disabled and non-disabled. As many as 95 per cent of us will experience notable disability at some point during our lives. If the Bible is to be truly light for those who cannot see, a voice to those who cannot hear and truth for those who have difficulty with understanding, we need to be constantly alert to these potential barriers.

In any case, it's not just people with disabilities who may struggle to access the life-changing message of the Bible. Most people have a Bible easily to hand, but many seem reluctant to open it. And even when they do, they face the challenge of knowing where to start reading its library of books in differing styles and from different eras. Let alone, the matter of understanding its message, couched in unfamiliar words and concepts.

Four hundred years ago the King James Version was created in response to growing demand for a Bible accessible to all. Let us use this celebration to commit ourselves to enabling everyone in society to access God's Word and experience him speaking directly to them, so that they too can experience the 'full life' found in Christ.

David Bendor-Samuel is Vice-Chairman of Churches for All, a consortium of Christian Disability charities and Director of Corporate Affairs for Prospects.

IT CHANGED MY WORLD:

'My daughter told me, "Mum, I have discovered the Word of God speaks to you".' **Mim**

Churches *for* All

Disabled people inspiring faith without limits

www.churchesforall.org

prospects

...access to life

www.prospects.org.uk

LYDIA TEBBUTT

READING THE BIBLE WITHOUT EYES

The Bible is available in so many versions and many attractive covers but what if you can't see it? The print in standard Bibles is typically rather small. How can those who are blind or losing their sight access the Bible and its life-giving message?

Reading the Bible with your ears

There are audio Bibles available from a number of publishers but with a standard cassette or CD audio Bible, it's just not possible to select a particular Bible verse or passage. Working in partnership with others, Torch has produced an audio Bible on disc, which revolutionizes Bible reading and study for people with sight loss. Using DAISY or the Digital Accessible Information SYstem it allows a very flexible approach to navigating the text. The audio recording is organized into 'levels' corresponding to books, chapters, groups of verses and finally, individual verses. DAISY players are widely available to people with sight loss. The DAISY Bible (TNIV) is £15.99 from Torch Trust or RNIB (Royal National Institute of Blind people). The Authorized Version should be available on DAISY disc in 2010.

Another popular audio Bible is 'Megavoice'. This is a palm-sized, hand-held, solar powered device, which is pre-loaded with a single Bible version and is available in several languages. Torch can supply these to people who are blind or partially sighted.

Aurora Ministries in the United States provides audio Bibles free to anyone with proof of blindness (www.audiobiblesfortheblind.org).

Torch, in conjunction with CWR and Scripture Union, also produce audio cassettes and DAISY versions of *Every Day With Jesus* and *Daily Bread* Bible reading notes, which include reading of the Bible passages mentioned.

Reading the Bible with your fingers

For people who can read Braille the following versions are available from the Torch Library: GNB, NIV, AV & RSV. The RNIB supplies several versions for sale or loan and the Lutheran Braille Workers in America produce an NIV free to blind and partially sighted people.

In conjunction with BRF and St John's Guild, Torch produces a Braille version of *New Daylight* Bible reading notes.

Reading the Bible with reduced sight

If you cannot read 12 point font size with corrective spectacles, then Torch's 24 point giant print might be useful to you. The NIV Bible is available to buy or borrow in individual volumes. The whole Bible can be purchased for £70 in hardback (19 volumes) or £35 in softcover (37 volumes). Alternatively, individual volumes can be purchased at £4.00 per volume and £1.00 per volume respectively.

Various large print Bibles, from 14 point to 22 point, are

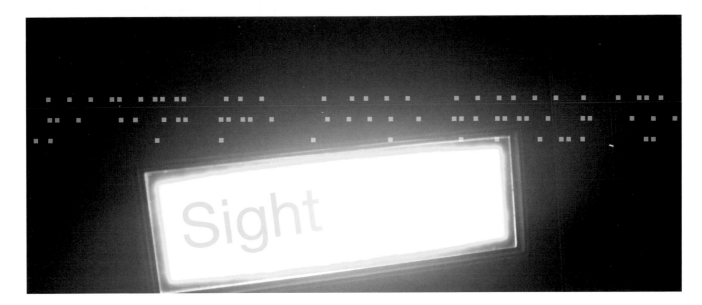

available from publishers such as Cambridge University Press, Scottish Bible Society and Gideons International.

Other Options

Although not all websites are accessible to blind and partially sighted people, the use of personal computers equipped with access software to go online, provides an increasingly important source of reading material.

Various organizations have websites which do make the Bible accessible to blind and partially sighted people e.g. Bible Gateway and International Bible Society.

The *Online Bible for PC* is easy to use, menu-driven, with screen helps, a search facility and extensive reference material and can be purchased from Torch at a special price for blind and partially sighted people.

More details of these and the other accessible Bibles can be found in *The Bible for Blind and Partially Sighted People* from the Torch Trust. To request a copy, in Braille, giant print or standard print ring 01858 438260 or email info@ torchtrust.org.

As well as the Bible, Torch Trust offers books from its lending library – the largest Christian library for blind people in the UK – in DAISY audio, Braille, giant print and cassette. There are over 3,000 titles covering theological, devotional, missionary, biographical and Christian leisure reading. Torch also produces a range of regular magazine publications, daily Bible reading notes, hymn and song books for people with sight loss.

Various organizations have websites which do make the Bible accessible to blind and partially sighted people.

WEBSITES

TORCH
vision for people with sight loss   **www.torchtrust.org**

Lydia Tebbutt is Literature Leader for Torch Trust

DAISY Bible TNIV
(Torch Trust, 2009)

Watcyn James

SPOTLIGHT

Tell us about a time when God spoke to you vividly and personally through the Bible.

Three passages have been central to my understanding of the immensity of the grace of God and the hope contained in the gospel.

The first is John 10:10 (ESV), 'I came that they may have life and have it abundantly.' This spoke to me at the beginning of my walk with God. It is the message that changed my life and underpins my preaching ministry and witness.

In recent years what has helped to keep the Bible fresh for you?

Isaiah 11:9, which sustained godly people in times of opposition, keeps recurring to me: 'They shall not hurt or destroy in all my holy mountain; for the earth shall be full of the knowledge of the Lord as the waters cover the sea' (ESV). Sometimes we get discouraged, but we have a promise that one day the whole world will be filled with the knowledge of God. Holding onto key promises helps us to hold onto the freshness of the Lord of heaven continually speaking into our lives.

What does your regular practice of Bible reading look like?

I find that systematically working through books of the Bible enables us to grasp the overarching themes of Scripture. Ideally, alongside this, a good, solid commentary, tackling a verse or a short passage at the time also helps us to wrestle with the text at a deeper level. The Word does not master us in a day – neither do we master the Word in a lifetime.

What would you say to a Christian who is struggling to read the Bible?

Don't give up! The third passage that encourages me is the theme of Colossians 1:15 ff. We have a pre-eminent, glorious Saviour, Jesus Christ, who is restoring the whole of

a fallen creation to himself. Through him alienated people can come into a relationship with God, reconciled, forgiven and awaiting fulfilment by his promise, 'if indeed you continue in the faith, stable and steadfast, not shifting from the hope of the gospel that you heard' (verse 23, ESV). Continuing, being stable and not shifting from the hope offered and procured in the gospel, draws us back to the Word.

What is your prayer for the Biblefresh initiative?

That churches across the UK joyfully rediscover a confidence in the transforming power of Scripture, as we are changed from glory into glory, as individuals and communities touched by grace.

Watcyn James is the Bible Society's Welsh Development Officer.

The Word does not master us in a day – neither do we master the Word in a lifetime.

JOE KAPOLYO

REMOVING CULTURAL BLINKERS

Cultural blinkers are an inevitable constituent of each person's make-up and identity. Any ethnic group's worldview and basic core values are captured in these blinkers. Each child born into that environment will inherit those blinkers and will predictably view life from those perspectives.

Cultural blinkers are rather like tinted spectacles through which we view life, the whole of life. The problem arises when any one person or more likely any one ethnic group makes the assumption that their particular set of cultural blinkers is normative for all people for all time. And anyone who does not view life or the Bible from that perspective is at best exotic and at worst deviant!

This is true of life in general as it is of our experience of life in the Christian community. When any Church grows to include people who come with different sets of cultural blinkers, the stage is set for serious culture clash and misunderstanding. The title of this article is somewhat misleading if it is understood to suggest that it is possible for any of us to divest ourselves of these blinkers. They are so deeply imbedded in us that they form an integral part of who we are and where we have come from. They are the distillation of the ways our forebears have developed to cope with life and to integrate new experiences into old ones. However, it is possible and necessary to minimize the parochial attitudes that can develop when we take our own view on life too seriously.

I spent my formative years as a Christian in a community where smoking cigarettes was not quite the 'unpardonable sin' but it clearly indicated that the smoker was either terribly backslidden or worse a non-Christian. While I lived in that community there were no arguments on that view of Christian holiness. I had the good fortune to visit Christian friends in their northern European home. After dinner every night my host would reach for his box of cigars and light up. I was very shocked and confused by this 'un-Christian' action! How can a Christian do this? There was no doubt in my mind that the brother was a Christian walking in step with the Spirit of the Lord. My journey in understanding cultural blinkers had begun!

At a personal level, I have been helped immensely to lose some of the parochialisms derived from my own 'rose-coloured Zambian glasses' by two factors. First, cross-cultural marriage; I owe a great debt of gratitude to my wife Anne and her Northern Irish background for helping me to see the other more clearly. In addition, I owe a similar debt to All Nations Christian College where my ministerial and missions skills were initially formed.

There are many ways to help us minimize the destructive effects of ethnocentric behaviour. Let me highlight just three:

TRAVEL: 'Umwana ashenda: atasha nyina ukunaya.' This is a Bemba proverb from north-eastern Zambia. A child who does not travel praises his mother's cooking. It is not possible to accurately appraise any action or activity without other points of comparison. Biblical theology is predicated on the cultural background of the theologian in question. European theologians with five hundred years of rationalism in their intellectual background will have largely bracketed out of their thought patterns stuff that Africans consider basic to daily living. Those African questions will not form a part of European biblical theology and the reverse is true. If we are to see the 'whole counsel of God' we must learn to travel, certainly in our minds, but also in a physical sense. The Christian Church will be the richer for these exchanges between people who wear different cultural blinkers.

CROSS-CULTURAL EXPERIENCES: Cross-cultural missions training, offered at leading institutions like All Nations Christian College, Redcliffe, London School of Theology, Oak Hill, ICC, etc., will help us to recognize our own boundedness in cultural matters and to appreciate the world views of other people and to learn from them ways of approaching God and expressing theology.

HUMILITY: A spirit of humility is vital if we are to shed our cultural blinkers. The Lord Jesus is the best example as always. His own 'cultural blinkers' of heaven are arguably the norm for all people for all time. But in relating to us and because of our needs he did not consider 'equality with God something to be grasped' (Philippians 2:6, NIV). He divested himself of the glory and majesty and entered into our experience wholly and stood where we stand and walked where we walk; he saw life from our perspective. He did this so that he could identify wholly with us in our state and that is why he is our Saviour and Redeemer.

Joe Kapolyo is Lead Minister at Edmonton Baptist Church, London. He is author of *The Human Condition* (IVP, 2005).

A SPIRIT OF HUMILITY IS VITAL IF WE ARE TO SHED OUR CULTURAL BLINKERS. THE LORD JESUS IS THE BEST EXAMPLE AS ALWAYS.

MY FAVOURITE BIBLE VERSE

PAM RHODES
TELEVISION PRESENTER

'Can a mother forget her nursing child? . . . But even if that were possible, I would not forget you! See, I have written your name on on the palms of my hands.' (Isaiah 49:15–16, NLT)

I find this verse so comforting! The thought that God knows, and has always known *me*, warts and all! Nothing I think or feel or do is beyond his understanding or love. However poorly I may think of myself, he has always been there, constant and parent-like. He rejoices when I am everything he hopes I will be. He is beside me when things go wrong and there's sadness and confusion. Because he's constant, I can be human.'

MATT VALLER

READING FROM THE
MARGINS

One of my favourite parts of the Bible is also one of its most absurd and provocative. It's Matthew 23:24 when Jesus accuses the Pharisees of straining a gnat but swallowing a camel. I have this image of myself sitting smugly in an armchair, empty cup of fresh tea in hand, a few gnats lolling groggily in my tea strainer and a giant camel protruding awkwardly from my mouth.

For Jesus, the Pharisees had missed the camel, the point of the Scriptures. Their place at the centre of religious society had somehow diverted their eyes to the gnatty periphery of their Bible. Jesus, a man on society's margins, was calling them back to its centre.

'The guys I spent time with were from horrendous backgrounds and like so many young people in that situation they were extremely angry,' explains Andy, who used to visit young offenders in prison as part of Youth for Christ's Reflex programme. 'That anger would come out in all sorts of violent ways, but when they heard David being angry at God – basically saying "Where were you when I needed you most?" – they could resonate with that. They wrote their own psalms using rap, which helped them to redirect that anger they felt. You'd have to put an 18-certificate on most of it, but it was such a profound and powerful experience to share those provocative prayers with them.'

I asked myself when was the last time my church's adult worship needed an 18-certificate? And had any of us read the Psalms with people on the margins? And were those two things related?

Valerie, on the other hand, has been reading the Bible with people in prison for most of the last decade. 'When I'm studying the Bible, and I'm doing that from their perspective, it just amazes me how I see passages in a different light,' she explains. We all want to hear some fresh word from God when we read. But to see this different light often requires us to get connected to people in our community who live different lives. Then we see with different eyes and hear the whisper of change.

Jo mentored Abi,* a teenage girl who lived in relative poverty with an abusive mother, an absent father, and strong behavioural issues which led to her exclusion from school. Abi had read the book of James and then Mark's gospel and one day she said to Jo, 'Jesus said the same as James about what it means to be a Christian.' She promptly flicked open her Bible and quoted James 1:27: 'Religion that God our Father accepts as pure and faultless is this: to look after orphans and widows in their distress' (NIV). Jo was stunned. This misunderstood girl, through all the challenges she faced, had captured the camel of Jesus' saying; she had found the weightier matters of 'justice, mercy and faithfulness' (Matthew 23:23). For Jo, 'Abi saw Jesus with a clarity that challenged me in how I worked out my faith.'

People living on the margins often find marginal things in the Bible they read. At least they are marginal according to the status quo. Abi's reaction to reading Mark and James shows just how powerful readings from the borders of society can be. Like Jesus himself, the eyes which read from the edge see with greater clarity the central concern of the Scriptures, concerns which without their insight remain hidden under the noses of the religious.

*not her real name

Matt Valler is National Youthwork Co-ordinator for Tearfund.

MY FAVOURITE BIBLE VERSE

LINVOY PRIMUS
PROFESSIONAL FOOTBALLER

' "I know the plans I have for you," says the Lord. "They are plans for good and not for disaster, to give you a future and a hope." '
(Isaiah 49:15–16, NLT)
When I first became a Christian, this verse was sent to me by a supporter, and as soon as I read it, I knew my future was taken care of.

ROSE DOWSETT

FROM ANOTHER
PERSPECTIVE

Generalizations are usually full of pitfalls, and in the world of religions that is certainly true. You will find exceptions to almost everything in this brief article!

'We have our own Scriptures'

Christianity is not unique in having its own sacred writings. All the major world faiths (and many smaller ones, along with many cults) have authoritative writings that shape their beliefs and practice, and that they regard as sacred. We share the Old Testament (OT) with Judaism, though Jews do not believe the Messiah has come and therefore reject the New Testament (NT) and the Christ to which it bears testimony. Islam accepts parts of both OT and NT, but believes the Koran supersedes them, that the prophet Mohammed supersedes Christ, and that the Christian Scriptures contain many errors. Hinduism and Buddhism have extensive sacred writings though it is often only religious scholars rather than most adherents who can easily read them.

Revelation

For most people outside the secular West, it is not a problem that sacred writings should have a supernatural origin, and be transmitted through some supernatural process. By contrast, many people in the West find the very concept of revelation impossible to accept; it does not sit easily with secularism and with the dominant scientific method based on reason and observation as the ground of truth. In some cases, for instance in Islam, it is believed that God (or some other Ultimate Being) directly dictated the writings to one human receptor who simply acted as scribe. This is different from the Christian understanding of revelation; the Bible has many human authors, inspired by the Holy Spirit so that their writings are

trustworthy, but retaining their own personalities, styles, and historical and cultural differences.

Respect or ignorance?

Most people have very little familiarity with sacred writings beyond their own faith. Some are respectful of sacred writings in general, without believing their teachings. Some adopt some themes but reject others: for instance, Gandhi, a Hindu, thought the Sermon on the Mount in the Christian NT was 'sublime'. Muslims don't understand why people and societies that call themselves Christian don't even attempt to live by the precepts of the Bible. This is offensive to them, as is the casual way in which people treat Bibles (the physical books) and the way in which 'Christian' societies tolerate blasphemy, permitting mockery of what should be sacred.

In most religions, the majority of adherents are not in fact very familiar with much of their own sacred writings, though most faiths have a minority with a good working knowledge of their books, which may or may not lead to radicalism and the persecution of those who are of a different faith. We recognize the problem of widespread biblical illiteracy among professing Christians, so we should not regard Christians as better informed about their faith than others, nor better shaped by orthodox Christian teaching.

Roadblocks to the Gospel

For many people in the world, their ethnic and/or national identity, and their corporate history, is strongly rooted in their religion. Questioning the reliability of their sacred writings, and introducing the Christian Bible, can thus profoundly challenge a person's identity at a deep level, not simply some abstract belief system. The Christian Bible is often identified, too, with western culture, perceived fairly in many parts of the world as very dissolute and immoral, and with painful past imperialism. The fact that there are many translations, and many arguments between Christians as to which is best, discredits the Bible in the eyes of some. Some of the non-Christian world is illiterate, or functionally illiterate, so oral transmission is very important. All this is before engaging with the contents of the Bible!

Bridges for the Gospel

The Holy Spirit does wonderful things when people read or hear the Christian Scriptures in their own language, and the difficulties should not deter us from sharing in faith God's Word whenever possible. People do not have to believe the whole Bible before coming to faith, but need to hear the stories of Jesus, who He was and is, and what he has done, the meaning of his death and resurrection. Buddhists may need first to learn of the Creator God before they can grasp the significance of Christ. Most religions have some element of wisdom literature, with an emphasis on moral, inner and spiritual values and behaviour, and that may be a connecting point. As Christians, we need to learn respectfully from friends of other faiths about what they believe, whilst being convinced of the uniqueness of the Lord Jesus Christ and of the Christian Gospel. It is good news, and God longs to see people of all ages, from every tribe and tongue and religion, come to saving faith in Christ.

IT CHANGED MY WORLD:

'I was raised in the church as a child and teenager but my impression of the Bible was that it was a general guideline for life – how to be a good person and how to treat others. I now realize that the Bible is far more. Scripture is indeed God's Word with which he brings us to salvation in Christ.' **Libby**

SALVATION

Rose Dowsett is a former missionary with OMF international, author, speaker, teacher at International Christian College, and Vice-Chairman of the WEA's Mission Commission.

EDDIE ARTHUR

WHERE IN THE
WORLD?

I felt pretty pleased with myself the first time I ever spoke to a church in French. At least I was pleased with myself until someone pointed out that I had confused *le foi* and *la foie* and had just given a ten minute talk on salvation through liver alone!

Trying to communicate or understand through a language that is not your own can be a real minefield, and the possibilities for confusion and embarrassment are endless. Just imagine, if you will, what it would be like not to have a Bible in English. Perhaps you could struggle through the Gospels on the back of some school French and memories from holiday, but what would happen when you tried to get to grips with Leviticus, or Romans?

We know that Christians struggle to set aside the time it takes to seriously study God's Word. If you add to that the burden of having to study in a foreign language, then many Christians would just give up trying to read their Bibles entirely. Not only that, but when people do get down to studying their Bibles, they may end up getting the wrong end of the stick entirely; like the Church leader I heard of who said that the Spirit descended on Jesus like a column of army ants because he misunderstood the word 'dove'. Little mistakes can change the sense of the passage and lead to the reinforcement of all sorts of wrong ideas about God (compare a feathery white dove and a column of marauding ants and see what they teach about the Holy Spirit!).

Now imagine that the French have the Bible, as well as the Dutch, Germans, Spanish and Italians but not the English. What does this say to you about the English language and about God's regard for the British people? God speaks French, but he doesn't speak English – he mustn't really care about the English. It is hard for us, speakers of a leading world language, to even imagine how it feels to have a language so marginalized that even God doesn't seem to speak it.

Across the world, there are two thousand languages, spoken by two hundred million people without a word of Scripture. If these people are going to have access to the Christian message at all right now it will be in a foreign language with all that means in terms of misunderstanding and confusion. But more importantly, as long as they can't hear the Scriptures in their own language, God remains a foreigner to them. The heart of the Christian message is about a God who reaches out to us and meets us at our point of need. This means his Word needs to be heard in the language of the hearers.

Bible translation is not simply about making the message easier to understand, it is about God coming to a people group and making his home with them. It is about him no longer being a foreigner to those who need to hear his voice.

There are people on every continent apart from Antarctica who don't have Scripture in their language. But the biggest concentration of need is in Central and West Africa, South East Asia and the Pacific Archipelago.

It is hard to put ourselves in the shoes of those who don't have the Scriptures, but we can do something to help change their situation.

Eddie Arthur is Executive Director at Wycliffe Bible Translators UK.

The **Bible:** The story everybody needs

wycliffe Bible translators

To learn more about worldwide Bible translation visit our website

wycliffe.org.uk

At the current rate of new Bible translation projects, work will have begun in each language where there is a need by the year **2041**. The average rate of documented new starts over the past 9 years is **71 languages per year**.

(Source: Researched by SIL International reported by Wycliffe International)

2,393* languages
with probable need of Bible translation

(Source: Researched by SIL International, reported by Wycliffe International)

6.5 billion
World population
(source: United Nations 2005)

6,909 languages
spoken in the world
(Ethnologue 16th Edition. 2008.
http://www.ethnologue.com)

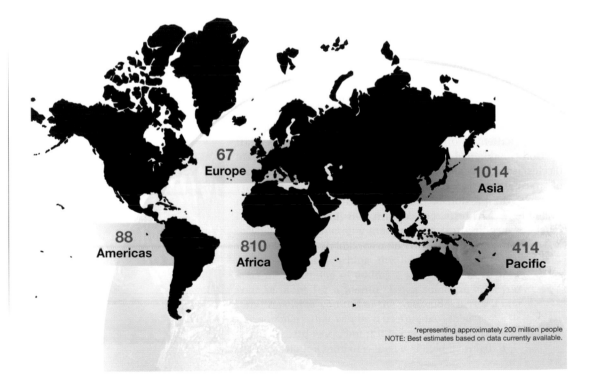

67
Europe

1014
Asia

88
Americas

810
Africa

414
Pacific

*representing approximately 200 million people
NOTE: Best estimates based on data currently available.

3. MY LOCAL BIBLE

You can now take the standard text of the Bible and customize the cover and helps inside to produce a local Bible. One idea to make use of this is to host a photography competition in your community on the theme of a particular Bible verse, with the prize of having the picture inserted into the Bible. Or you could make localized study notes – so imagine an Oxford Bible that relates the stories of the Oxford Martyrs or C.S. Lewis's conversion – or a Merseyside Bible that demonstrates how both Everton and Liverpool FC were founded by local churches. Or imagine your town or village offering a Bible with testimonies and pictures from local people that you give out during Lent or a mission week.

If you would like more information email info@authenticmedia.co.uk.

4. HOUSE GROUP QUESTIONS

This is the simple idea of asking at least one question each time you meet that will help the group to think about how they will translate the truth they have been discussing from God's Word into something helpful to talk about with friends and colleagues. For example, a house group looking at God's faithfulness in Psalm 139 might ask a question like, 'A colleague at work has recently found out his son has leukaemia, is there anything from tonight's study that could be a help to him?' Or 'How would you summarize the key points of tonight in language that someone who is exploring the Christian faith for the first time might understand?' This approach can add a missionary facet to the study and force participants to translate the message they have been hearing in house group to the language of the street, office and neighbourhood. This discipline helps us to understand the Bible more clearly in the

first place; as a catchphrase used at the London School of Theology would put it, 'In order to explain something simply you must understand it profoundly.'

5. WHAT'S IN A NAME?

How about trying to consider a non-Christian audience if you have the responsibility for constructing the titles for the church sermon series? Christians will come to church services whatever the title of the series, but you might just help someone else attend if you choose them a little more carefully. And it also helps the congregation to make the right connections between the text and their daily contexts. For example, here's a set of sermon outlines I used for a series on Matthew's gospel (which later turned into a book called *Dysciples*):

Dissatisfied: Why I feel I am going nowhere (Matthew 4:12-22)

Despairing: Why I shout at God (Matthew 8:23-27)

Disoriented: Why I won't step out of my comfort zone (Matthew 14:22-34)

Disgruntled: Why I struggle with Jesus' teaching (Matthew 15:1-20)

Dismissive: Why I've heard it all before (Matthew 15:29 – 16:12)

Disconnected: Why I feel such a hypocrite (Matthew 16:13-28)

Distant: Why God seems out of reach (Matthew 17:1-11)

Disappointed: Why I can't move mountains (Matthew 17:14:23).

Over to you . . .

6. ECHO THE STORY

Michael Novelli translates Bible stories from the text of Scripture into a format that is easy to remember, and then spends his youth group meetings telling the story, asking the hearers to retell what they've heard and then think their way into the stories they have just retold. Translating the Bible from a written text into an oral story helps us to connect with the Bible in a new way for us, but in a way that would have been very familiar to the first hearers of the Bible. Read more in the Experience section or go to www.echothestory.com for more details.

In order to explain something simply you must understand it profoundly

7. YOUTUBE IT

I gave my Sunday school class a video-making challenge: to translate the first two chapters of Genesis into a stop-motion film. All you need is a digital camera per group and a computer to put the creations together and you are away! Basically stop-motion is the same technique used by animators like Nick Park in his Wallace and Gromit films. You take a photo, then make a slight move to the scene and then take another photo. We have made movies with people standing really still, using Lego bricks and using toy cars. It is great fun and gives some really cool visual results. The artistic nature of the project forced my group of 9- to 13-year-olds to try and think through the structure of the Genesis account and then come up with creative ways of making the films. The Sunday school class posted the videos online and then told their mates at school what they had done. We had some nice comments back from their RE teachers too. It's cheap and cheerful, but helps a generation of screenagers engage with Scripture in new ways. If you do make a movie, post it on Youtube and send us a link so we can feature it on the Biblefresh website.

8. TOTAL RECALL

If we are working through a series in a book of the Bible in our church services or house group, we will often try and recall as a group as much of the Bible text as we can from the section we studied last week. For example, in a recent series we worked through Paul's letter to the Colossian church, so at the beginning of each house group, we would try and remember our way starting from Paul's greeting to the church up to the point we had reached the previous week. This forced us to think through the overall argument of the letter and helped us to avoid twisting small snippets of the letter out of their original context. One elderly member of our church got really excited by this, as she normally really struggles to remember things; the discipline of trying to recall the letter had helped her to see the big picture of Colossians for the first time and she was able to reel off quotation after quotation, nearly verbatim.

9. PRAYER TRANSLATION

Another powerful way of translating the Bible is to turn the text you are studying into a prayer. Recently in a Bible study of Revelation 21, when John describes how when the heavens and the earth are renewed and 'there will be no more death or mourning or crying or pain, for the old order of things has passed away' (NIV), I asked people to pray this in their own words. I was really moved when a group I was working with prayed, 'Lord Jesus, thank you that one day there will be no more displaced people, violence against women, hungry children, oil slicks, bulimia or suicide. Lord, help us to give people a taste of that future today.' Another group I was working with turned Psalm 103 into a personal prayer – each person prayed out one part of the passage that they wanted to express in praise back to God.

10. NO BIBLE SUNDAY

As well as translating the Word into meaning in our contexts, let's not forget those who don't even have the Bible in their own language in the first place. To inspire your church to get behind the Bible translation project in Burkina Faso mentioned in previous pages, why not make use of some of the resources produced by Wycliffe Bible Translators to give your church a flavour of what it is like to be bereft of Scripture. One idea is to hold a No Bible Sunday, in order to help you to value the Bible through its absence. There are dozens of other creative ideas – including for youth and children – which highlight the importance of Bible translation (www.wycliffe.org.uk/resources).

Krish Kandiah is Executive Director: Churches in Mission at the Evangelical Alliance and author of *How to Save a Life* (Authentic, 2009).

NOW I KNOW I MATTER

EXPERIENCING THE WORD

BIBLE EXPERIENCES

GERARD KELLY

EVERYTHING WE BRING

Everything we bring
To this place
Finds a place here

Every case that we carry can be consigned here
Every load we are lifting can be left
Every secret we are slaves to can be spoken here
Every terror that torments us can be told

There is room here for anguish
For the agony of abandonment
There is ground here for grieving
For the weeping wounds of loss

In this circle of safety
At this fireside of faith
There is space for story and song
There is room for revelation and renewal
Here is hope
And healing
Here is forgiveness
And freedom
Here is connection
And correction
And coming to our senses
At this source
Whose depths are never ending

This river
That will never run dry
At this table
Whose banquet of abundance
Knows no bounds

No wrong
Is too wrong
To be righted here
No tragedy too twisted
To be turned
For everything we bring
To this place
Finds a place here
And every load we are lifting can be left

www.blessnet.eu
www.twitter.com/twitturgies

Gerard Kelly is Senior
Pastor of Crossroads
Church, Amsterdam
and Co-Director of the
Bless Network.
He is author of
*Intimate with the
Ultimate* (Authentic,
2009).

ALLY GORDON

BUT IS IT
ART?

Stroll around an art gallery today and you never know what you might get. In the last five years contemporary British artists have exhibited dead sheep, unmade beds, self-portraits sculpted from frozen blood and light switches that turn themselves on and off. Today we are as likely to consider the artistic merits of a pickled shark in the same breath as a painting by Rembrandt or Picasso.

But is it art and what does God make of it all? Does the Bible have anything to say about these new forms of art?

The definitions of art have been blurring ever since Marcel Duchamp placed his urinal in the 1917 Society of Independent Artists exhibition in Paris. We could blame our general confusion about art on the collapse of modernist values, the death of the author, the loss of meta-narratives and all that post-structuralist, post-modern, post-whatever but this is not to say new forms of contemporary art are without value to God, 'for the earth is the Lord's and everything in it' (Psalm 24:1) and 'everything God created is good, and nothing is to be rejected' (1 Timothy 4:4, NIV).

The Bible is full of guidance for those who make art or want to engage with it for God's glory. In the broadest sense of 'art', the Bible is a magnificent artwork in its own right. Think of the poetry of the Psalms or the apocalyptic imagery of

Revelation (better than any Hollywood epic!), the nationalistic poetry of 1 and 2 Chronicles or the beautiful artefacts of the Exodus tabernacle. Bono of U2 described the psalmist David as 'one of the greatest blues writers of all time'.[1] David himself uses artistic language to describe God's Word as water to the soul and 'honey to my mouth' (Psalm 119:103). When was the last time you read the Psalms like great poetry, allowing the Word of God to drip off your lips like sweet-tasting honey?

Not only is the Bible a great work of art but within its pages are descriptions of great artists such as Bezalel (Exodus 31) who made the art for the tabernacle and was filled with 'skill, ability and knowledge in all kind of crafts' and Moses who sculpted the bronze snake in Numbers 21. We might even consider the actions of the prophets as a kind of performance art such as Ezekiel's lie-down which was a form of Old Testament theatre (Ezekiel 4) or the binding of Paul's hands by the prophet Agabus as a form of conceptual illustration (Acts 21:10,11). None of these actions would be out of place in a gallery today and they appear to tick all the right boxes to be considered as art.

Art as we know it today didn't exist in biblical times but this is not to say the Bible has nothing to say about contemporary art. Being creative is the first thing God chooses to record about himself in the Bible, 'In the beginning God created' (Genesis 1:1) and his creation was 'very good' (Genesis 1:31). From the beginning God is interested in the aesthetic dimension of his creation, making the trees 'pleasing to the sight' as well as 'good for food' (Genesis 2:9). In Genesis we find a plethora of creative arts including poetry (Genesis 2:23), music (Genesis 4:21) and even town planning (Genesis 4:17).

Since we are made in the image of God, all aspects of his creation are available for us to enjoy and have dominion over. The Christian artist's task is to steward the visual aspects of our culture just as Adam was placed in the Garden of Eden to 'work it and take care of it' (Genesis 2:15). Paul writes, 'Whatever you do, work at it with all your heart, as working for the Lord and not for men' (Colossians 3:23). We are to graft hard in our art to reflect the greatness of our Creator God in whose image we are made.

The simple act of making art can give great glory to God because it is part of his design for his people but this is not to say that all art is pleasing to God. In the Bible God's anger burned against the Israelite people for making a gold sculpture of a calf because they had placed their trust for salvation in it rather than him (Exodus 32). Even Moses' bronze sculpture of a snake became idolatrous to the people, despite being designed as a symbol of God's healing and deliverance from the venomous snakes in the desert. The fact that God gives creative gifts to those who love him as well as those who don't is a sign of his common grace to all humanity. God has given extraordinary gifts of art to those who don't serve him even though many have chosen to use their gifts to make art that opposes him.

As a Christian and an artist I am encouraged by the role artists play in the new creation. As bearers of salt and light through visual means we can reflect something of the hope of Christ as well as mirroring the despair of a fallen world. We look forward to Christ's return and the establishment of a new creative culture when God will wipe every tear from our eyes and proclaim, 'I am making everything new' (Revelation 21:5).

Ally Gordon is an artist and co-ordinator of UCCF: Interface Arts.

Art & Soul: Signposts for Christians in the Arts by Hillary Brand and Adrienne Chaplin (Piquant, 2001).

'As a Christian and an artist I am encouraged by the role artists play in the new creation.

CREATION

STEVE HOLMES

'ALL THAT YOU CAN'T LEAVE BEHIND': THE BIBLE IN POPULAR MUSIC

I don't often get genuinely annoyed listening to the radio news in the morning. A little while ago, however, it happened. I was half-asleep, still, waking up to Radio 5. There was some discussion about a cover of Leonard Cohen's *Hallelujah* just released by some X-factor winner, which was roughly 0.01 per cent as good as Jeff Buckley's earlier cover of the same song.

The interviewer quoted the second verse, which recalls David seeing Bathsheba bathing, and Samson surrendering to Delilah, being tied up, and having his hair cut. The interviewee, a pop music journalist, clearly took this (tying up and hair cutting) as a reference to some odd sexual perversion, and was rather embarrassed. No one in the studio seemed to recognize the biblical references, or the brilliant way that Cohen wove together the two stories into a reflection on how lust can destroy God's gifts in us. A great song, meditating on biblical themes, first murdered by the cover artist, then misunderstood by the interview. I was angry.

For people on the cutting edge of a culture that believes it has left the Bible behind long ago, the writers of our popular songs are strangely unable to escape the text. For some, it is simply that biblical phrases are everywhere in the English language: Coldplay's citing of the Lord's Prayer ('Kingdom Come'; 'Yes') does not, I suppose, mean very much. But for others Bible quotation is far more extensive and deliberate. Cohen does it with striking insight; Franz Ferdinand with savage irony ('Auf Asche'; 'The Fallen'); Depeche Mode or Sinead O'Connor with angry, if fascinated, rejection. Again and again, however, Scripture is cited.

Pop and rock musicians are not often devoted, not converts, but they just cannot leave this text alone. There are preachers who quote the Bible less often than U2 or Bob Dylan! Bruce Springsteen or Runrig do it less, but seem just as fascinated by the text. It seems that the words of Scripture remain powerful even for non-Christian musicians. They are a call to something beyond and unknown, intensely attractive if also frightening for some; beguiling, if repulsive, for others.

We Christians might worry about this cultural appropriation of the Bible, wanting to police the use of the text to make sure it is done properly. We should remember C.H. Spurgeon, however: when asked to defend the Bible, he responded, 'I would sooner defend an uncaged lion!' People struggling with the words of Scripture in public should not worry us. Rather we should encourage them, and their hearers, to struggle more – like Jacob at the river Jabbok, those who struggle with God may be wounded, but they may also be transformed.

And, like Caiaphas, they may also speak – or sing – more than they know. Depeche Mode wrote 'Personal Jesus' to mock the faith of Christians that God might intervene in response to our prayers; at the end of his life, riddled with cancer, Johnny Cash covered the song on his *American IV* CD, and made it a heartfelt confession of his faith in God's presence and help. For Depeche Mode, 'reach out and touch' was a cynical statement of an impossibility; for Cash it was a prayer that had been answered before and would be answered again. The uncaged lion has a habit of winning its fights.

Photo courtesy of hds

Steve Holmes is Senior Lecturer in Theology, Director of Teaching and Deputy Head of School of Divinity at the University of St Andrews. He is co-editor of *What are We Waiting For?* (Paternoster, 2009).

THERE ARE PREACHERS WHO QUOTE THE BIBLE LESS OFTEN THAN U2 OR BOB DYLAN!

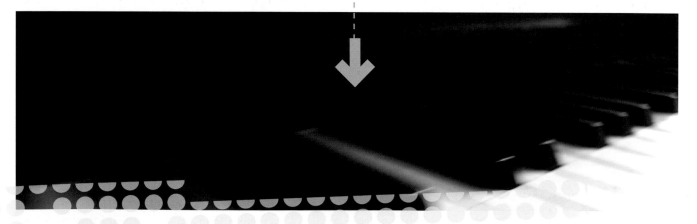

TONY WATKINS

AND THE WORD BECAME FILM

Film is a global medium, but its origins are in western culture, which has been decisively shaped by Christianity for centuries. Despite rampant secularism, the Bible is still something of a touchstone for our society. Directly or indirectly, it impacts writers, film-makers and others. There is something about its story which people still find compelling. It seems that our culture just cannot let go of the ideas within it – even when they disagree with them.

Some films specifically tell parts of the Bible story. The earliest full-length biblical film was probably Sidney Olcott's *From the Manger to the Cross* in 1912. Hundreds of others have been made since, including classics like Cecil B. DeMille's film *The Ten Commandments*. This 1956 epic was, in fact, his second look at this subject; he had previously made a silent film version in 1923. Charlton Heston's Moses is an iconic figure, still instantly recognizable, even among younger generations who haven't seen the film. Given the drama of Moses' story, it's surprising that there are not more movies about him. The most notable is DreamWorks Animation's *The Prince of Egypt* (1998), though there are plans for a new film about him in the style of *300*. There's no surprise that film-makers like the Samson and Delilah story: as well as an enigmatic flawed hero, there's plenty of violence and sensuality to spice things up. Victor Mature and Hedy Lamarr played the title roles in DeMille's 1949 epic, which is the best-known of all Samson films.[1]

Of course, Jesus is the focus of most explicitly biblical films. George Stevens's colossally expensive movie, *The Greatest Story Ever Told* (1965), was just one of many Bible epics from that era including DeMille's *King of Kings* (1961). Two notable examples from the previous decade were Henry Koster's *The Robe* (1953) and William Wyler's *Ben Hur* (1959).

Perhaps surprisingly, biblical films still get made, *The Passion of the Christ* (2004) being the obvious example. Astonishingly, Catherine Hardwicke's 2006 film *The Nativity Story* seems to be the first feature film which concentrates on Jesus' birth, though another, *Mary Mother of Christ*, is in production. The Bible (especially the gospels) is difficult ground for film-makers, though: it's hard to get right and easy to offend. Scorsese's *The Last Temptation of Christ* (1988) had some very positive aspects to its portrayal of Jesus, but also some deeply objectionable ones.

Many more films refer to the Bible, rather than portraying it. Passion play films like *Jesus of Montreal* (1989), for example, aren't primarily telling the story of Jesus, but they include elements of it. Norman Stone's *Man Dancin'* (2003) is a powerful, but sadly little-known, example. *Life of Brian* (1979) isn't about Jesus at all, but is set in the same historical context in order to satirize religion's shortcomings. Some uses of the Bible in films are natural, because they're about religious people, like Eric Liddell (Ian Charleson) in *Chariots of Fire* (1981). There's a nice exchange in *Dead Man Walking* (1995) when a prison guard approvingly quotes 'an eye for an eye' to Sister Helen (Susan Sarandon) when she visits a prisoner on death row. 'Know what else it asks for?' she asks in response. 'Death as a punishment for adultery, prostitution, homosexuality, trespass upon sacred ground, profaning the Sabbath and contempt of parents.' The guard gives up, saying, 'I ain't gonna get into no Bible quotin' with no nun, 'cause I'm gonna lose.'

When the Bible is used in unexpected contexts, it's important to think about why. *Gattaca* (1997) starts with Ecclesiastes 7:13 – 'Consider God's handiwork; who can straighten what he hath made crooked?' The film explores the dangers of genetic engineering, suggesting that it is 'playing God'. Other examples include a title card quoting John 9:24–26 in *Raging Bull* (1980), and *The X-Files: I Want to Believe* quoting Proverbs 25:2. Sometimes, film-makers are just having fun making biblical connections, as with the frequent references to Exodus 8:2 in *Magnolia* (1999). And then there's the misquoting of the Bible, most famously by Jules in *Pulp Fiction* (1994) when he completely mangles Ezekiel 25:17. It's part of the humour that his 'quotation' is mostly invention.

Whenever the Bible is referred to, we should reflect on why and how it has been used. Whether it's used well or badly, it opens up an opportunity for us to talk about what it really says and why we need to listen to it.

Tony Watkins is a speaker, writer and editor, working mainly with Damaris Trust. He is author of *Focus: The Art and Soul of Cinema* (Damaris, 2007).

 IT CHANGED MY WORLD:

'I used to be a very bitter and angry person. We did a Bible study on John's gospel. When we were finished my daughter said, "You have become a much nicer mum". It has transformed the whole family.' **Nicole**

TRANSFORMED

JEZ CARR

ENGAGING THE
ARTISTIC PERSONALITY

The mosaic of church community has the potential to be rich and colourful: in each of us, God has planted diverse elements of his character for which we are ambassadors.

By representing the sacred things we hold dear, we lead each other to engage holistically in the life to which God calls us. The academic leads us in thinking rigorously, the activist in putting our faith into action, and so on. But what is the artist's ambassadorial role? As a starting point, let me use some inexcusably broad brushstrokes to describe some traits which are common to most artists.

The artist has a complex relationship with truth, dominated by unseen interactions of feelings and imagination. Presenting propositions is not enough. This subconscious activity is associated with introspection and emotional turbulence, issuing in a high valuing of personal authenticity, especially regarding our experience of brokenness. Artists tend to be suspicious of ideas which jar with their felt reality, especially when the incongruity is left unexpressed. Of course these are traits we all share, but they are often generally a bigger deal for artists.

Artists are therefore ambassadors of authenticity and imagination. They lead us in being what we are, being seen as God sees us, not as we want to be seen, and therefore in being credible in a postmodern world. And they lead us towards a holistic, imaginative engagement with Scripture, enabling us to appreciate the transcendent, unfinished yet over-familiarized mysteries of faith. Without art, God gets smaller, hope gets fainter, and the gospel goes stale.

Historically, the church has treated artists with some suspicion: an imaginative engagement with truth is necessarily ambiguous, and that presents doctrinal dangers. An authenticity, which dwells on the brokenness of life, has often been perceived as pouring water on Christian joy and hope. However, other people in the church should be able to prevent these perceived dangers from growing teeth, without undermining the artistic contribution. I'm not just talking about using art as a point of reflection after the 'meat' of the sermon, or as a conversation starter – though it can do those well. I'm talking about integrating these artistic values into the whole way we approach the Bible (which is, don't forget, saturated with art).

Let's take as an example the story of the plagues. Here we learn that nothing and no one can rival God's power. Riveted yet? I didn't think so. You knew that. But God wants you to know it in a way that makes ten plagues worthwhile. Why else did God bother with all those plagues rather than just skipping to the last one? God wanted to recapture the Israelites' imaginations. Everything about Pharaoh declared him to be god – every Israelite sense was left tingling with Pharaoh's divinity. Moses couldn't just tell them that God was stronger and march them to freedom – that would be no match for Pharaoh's propaganda machine. God wanted to free the people in a way that overwhelmed their tingling senses and gave them a story to tell their grandchildren when they too were enslaved to other gods – a story that could fight imagination with imagination. When we preach about the plagues, we can't just get up and say the obvious – the gods that enslave us are too

Jez Carr is a pianist and producer.

powerful for that. We have to feel Pharaoh's majesty and God's dramatic acts of humiliation. We need to see Granddad's eyes red and wide as he tells the story. Then maybe, as we face our Pharaohs, our imaginations too will be captured by God.

PHIL COLLINS

THE WORD'S A
STAGE

We have the exciting task of bringing the Bible to life. So what do we need? We need creativity at the heart of our communication. Without creativity we are in danger of failing. It is so important to communicate the Bible with an inspiring innovative style, giving animation to the Bible in the twenty-first century. Many of us as young teenagers endured boring and tedious lessons at school; my worst nightmare was 2.30 p.m. in the afternoon enduring a certain physics lesson! The difference between killing a subject and bringing it alive is the enthusiastic creativity that the teacher employs: we've all seen Robin Williams's stroke of genius in *Dead Poet's Society*. Zero creativity equals zero impact.

So how critical is it to bring the maximum impact from the way we share Scripture? Like all great theatre productions or films, we need a beginning, a middle and an end. When aiming to dramatize the Bible in your local church community, don't forget that the Bible is full of wonderful stories, characters, interaction and visual effects all wonderfully described for us by the various biblical writers. Don't let the way you dramatize it cloud the essence of the truth of the story.

First of all gather a group of willing volunteers who want to have a lot of fun and laughter, and whose attitude is that of humility and service. It is, however, very important that this group has a leader or even a director, so that the group does not descend into artistic chaos! This person can capture the ideas of the group and help shape the presentation. There is always a danger with creative people, of this exercise becoming intense and the whole creative process becomes a stressful experience. We must remember that energy and enjoyment brings the story alive. Do not be afraid to use existing materials, those little sketches and ideas that are all over the Internet. Take it, shape it and develop it, let your imagination run away with itself. Helpful resources such as *The Message, The Dramatized Bible*, or *The Word on the*

Street are great. They can often give us a framework to begin from but, be aware, avoid complex themes and lengthy monologues; keep it simple, interesting and colourful. Use as many props as possible to help characterization . . . a hat changes everything. Take the Bible story and then make it relevant to your audience. So, if the beginning needs to be fun and full of enthusiasm, with a clear simple theme, the middle contains the development of the ideas.

Take the characters from the Bible and bring them alive. A very good way is to take a little-known biblical character and give them a large voice that guides the story through. We recently visited seventy primary schools with Saltmine Theatre Company. We adapted the well-known story of Joseph. To help bring the story alive, we super-sized his brother Rueben as a hilarious link to the narrative. Rueben, the funny little character with the bent glasses, guided Joseph through the story. So make a minor character become major . . . this in turn gives you more creative licence. Don't be afraid to add modern references either, we threw in raps, audience participation, contemporary jokes and items from current celebrity culture,

all the time connecting the Bible story to the audience and their world. Don't feel trapped by the biblical period. There is always a danger in performing straight from the text that we end up simply reading it or it becomes predictable from the beginning to the end. Predictability kills good theatre. This middle period needs lots of time. Avoid rushing rehearsals at all costs - don't complete your production on the Sunday morning before the service!

So we need to gather our enthusiastic few, give ourselves creative licence and finally, think about the 'big ending'. It's always good to end on a bang.

People remember how things begin and how they finish. I have witnessed many creative ends - funny little songs, an explosion or a well-timed, clear ending sentence - but we must always remember that it is the clarity of the story that needs to flow. People love stories, and if we tell a good story with enthusiastic people, use colour and props, embrace contemporary themes and ideas, and have a clear ending . . . we will make the Bible live to a generation who have little or no understanding. Enjoy!

Phil Collins is CEO of the Saltmine Trust.

An Angel's Delight DVD by David Robinson (Saltmine).

Three Wise Men and a Baby and Other Seasonal Sketches by David Robinson (Saltmine/ Authentic, 2007).

The Mystery and the Passion: Creating Holy Theatre by Richard Hasnip (Saltmine/ Authentic, 2009).

Saltmine

MY FAVOURITE BIBLE VERSE

BARONESS COX
HUMANITARIAN AID RELIEF TRUST

'I command you – be strong and courageous! Do not be afraid or discouraged. For the Lᴏʀᴅ your God is with you wherever you go.' (Joshua 1:9, NLT)

As my work with people suffering oppression and persecution frequently takes me to dangerous places, I find this message a source of encouragement and a reminder of God's presence.

Stephen Gaukroger

Tell us about a time when God spoke to you vividly and personally through the Bible.

A couple of years ago I thought I was being called into a new area of ministry. God used Genesis 12 and the story of Abraham ('Go to the land which I will show you') to confirm that it was right to take this step even though I didn't know exactly what the shape of the future ministry would look like.

In recent years what has helped to keep the Bible fresh for you?

I have been one of the series editors for the Crossway Bible Guides for the last ten years. Every time I receive a manuscript dealing with the next Bible book I find new insights & helpful challenges in this material. Most of the Bible has been covered by this series and so I've had the opportunity to have my Bible knowledge strengthened by the wisdom of a wide range of Bible teachers.

What does your regular practice of Bible reading look like?

My wife & I pray together each morning. I read the Bible at different points in the day and sometimes set aside a whole afternoon or morning to read through a Bible book at one sitting.

What would you say to a Christian who is struggling to read the Bible?

Sometimes it helps to read the Bible with other people in a prayer partnership or triplet. Share your struggle with a trusted Christian leader. Don't feel guilty when you get it wrong – and don't give up!

What is your prayer for the Biblefresh initiative?

That God will help churches and individuals fall in love with the Scriptures all over again and make the Bible central to all we believe and the way we live and order our church life.

Share your struggle with a trusted Christian leader. Don't feel guilty when you get it wrong – and don't give up!

Stephen Gaukroger is the Director of Clarion Trust International and former President of the Baptist Union. He is author of *Discovering Daniel* (Crossway, 2005).

SPOTLIGHT

EUGENE H. PETERSON

THE HOLY COMMUNITY
AT TABLE WITH HOLY SCRIPTURE

'I went to the angel and told him to give me the little scroll; and he said to me, 'Take it, and eat; it will be bitter to your stomach, but sweet as honey in your mouth.' And I took the little scroll from the hand of the angel and ate it; it was sweet as honey in my mouth, but when I had eaten it my stomach was made bitter.' (Revelation 10:9–10, NRSV)

Does that get our attention? St John is a commanding figure. He was pastor of marginal, politically and economically powerless Christians in a society in which their commitment to following Christ branded them as criminals of the state. His task was to keep their identity focused and their lives Spirit-filled, their discipleship ardent, their hope fresh against formidable odds – the living, speaking, acting Jesus front and centre in their lives. He didn't settle for mere survival, throwing them a plank to hang onto in the storm; he wanted them to live, really live – outlive every one around them. This is what prophets and pastors and writers do, and it is never easy. No easier now than it was for John.

It was in the course of the apocalyptic extravaganza that John is so famous for – these wildly boisterous, rambunctious, and celebrative visions that came to him one Sunday morning as he was worshipping on the prison island of Patmos – just as he was approaching the midpoint in the sequence of vision-messages, that he saw a gigantic angel, one foot planted in the ocean and the other on the continent, with a book in his hand. From this comprehensive land-and-sea pulpit the angel was preaching from the book, a sermon explosive with thunder. This was a sermon no one would sleep through! John started to write down what he was hearing – he'd never heard a sermon like this one – but was then told not to. A voice told John to take the book from the huge angel, this God-Messenger preaching from his world-straddling pulpit. And so he did, he walked up to the angel and said, 'Give me the book.' The angel gave it to him, but then said, 'Here it is; eat it. Eat this book. Don't just take notes on the sermon. Eat the book.' And John did it. He put away his notebook and pencil. He picked up his knife and fork. He ate the book.

The imagery, as is all the imagery in St John's Revelation, is complex, a fusion of images from Moses and the Prophets and Jesus.

This vision of the preaching angel is full of reverberating resonances. But what appears most immediate and obvious is that the mighty angel is preaching from the Bible, the Holy Scriptures. The book that John ate was the Bible, or as much of the Bible as was written at that time. The word 'book' (Greek *biblion*, which arrives in our language as 'Bible') suggests that the message God gives to us has meaning, plot, and purpose. Writing a book involves ordering words in a purposeful way. These words make sense. We do not come to God by guesswork: God reveals himself. These scriptural words reveal the Word that created heaven and earth; they reveal the Word that became human flesh in Jesus for our salvation. God's Word is written, handed down, and translated for us so that we can enter the plot. We hold these Bibles in our hands and read them so that we can listen and respond to these creating and saving words and get in, firsthand, on the creating and saving. The act of eating the book means that reading is not a merely objective act, looking at the words and ascertaining their meaning. Eating the book is in contrast with how most of us are trained to read books – develop a cool objectivity that attempts to preserve scientific or theological truth by eliminating as far as possible any personal participation that might contaminate the meaning. But none of us starts out reading that way. I have a granddaughter right now who eats books. When I am reading a story to her brother, she picks another off of a stack and chews on it. She is trying to get the book inside her the quickest way she knows, not through her ears, but through her mouth. She doesn't make fine distinctions between ear and mouth – any opening will do to get it inside her. But soon she'll go to school and be taught that that's not the way to go about it. She'll be taught to get answers out of her book. She'll learn to read books in order to pass examinations, and having passed the exams, put the book on the shelf and buy another.

But the reading that John is experiencing is not of the kind that equips us to pass an examination. Eating a book takes it all in, assimilating it into the tissues of our lives. Readers become what they read. If Holy Scripture is to be something other than mere gossip about God, it must be internalized. Most of us have opinions about God that we are not hesitant to voice. But just because a conversation (or sermon or lecture) has the word 'God' in it, does not qualify it as true. The angel does not instruct St John to pass on information about God; he commands him to assimilate the Word of God so that when he does speak, it will express itself artlessly in his syntax just as the food we eat, when we are healthy, is unconsciously assimilated into our nerves and muscles and put to work in speech and action. Words – spoken and listened to, written and read – are intended to do something in us, give health and wholeness, vitality and holiness, wisdom and hope. Yes, eat this book.

St John, as mentioned earlier, wasn't the first biblical prophet to eat a book as if it were a peanut butter sandwich. Six hundred years earlier Ezekiel had been given a book and commanded to eat it (Ezekiel 2:8 – 3:3). Ezekiel's contemporary, Jeremiah, also ate God's revelation, his version of the Holy Bible (Jeremiah 15:16). Ezekiel and Jeremiah, like John, lived in a time in which there was widespread pressure to live by a very different text than the one revealed by God in these Holy Scriptures. The diet of Holy Scripture for all three of them issued in sentences of tensile strength, metaphors of blazing clarity, and a prophetic life of courageous suffering. If we are in danger (which we certainly are) of succumbing to the widespread setting-aside of the Holy Scriptures and the replacing of them with the text of our own experience – our needs and wants and feelings – for authoritative direction in our actual day-by-day living, these three rough-and-tumble prophets – John, Ezekiel, Jeremiah – responsible for the spiritual formation of God's people in the worst of times (Babylonian exile and Roman persecution) ought to be able to convince us of their gut-level necessity: Yes, eat this book.

The Christian community has expended an enormous amount of energy and intelligence and prayer in learning how to 'eat this book' after the manner of John on Patmos, Jeremiah in Jerusalem, and Ezekiel in Babylon.[1] We don't have to know all of it to come to the Table, but it helps to know some of it, especially since so many of our contemporaries treat it as a mere aperitif. The strong angel's command is also an invitation. Come to the Table and eat this book, for every word in the book is intended to do something in us, give health and wholeness, vitality and holiness to our souls and body.

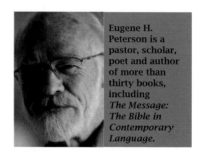

Eugene H. Peterson is a pastor, scholar, poet and author of more than thirty books, including *The Message: The Bible in Contemporary Language*.

Taken from *Eat This Book: A Conversation in the Art of Spiritual Reading* by Eugene H. Peterson (Hodder & Stoughton, 2006). Used by permission.

JANE HOLLOWAY

TAKE IT AND EAT

It's a sobering place to find ourselves as the UK Church at the start of the twenty-first century, adrift from the Word of God. As fewer and fewer Christians regularly take time to spend with God reading the Bible, fewer and fewer make time to pray. Prayer has been pushed to the sidelines.

Biblefresh not only gives us a wonderful opportunity to stop, read and study the Bible again but it also allows us access to the best manual on prayer there is!

The Bible teaches us about the practice and reality of prayer, as it contains thousands of examples of how God's people prayed and what they prayed for. We learn about the struggles in prayer, the sacrifice of prayer and when prayer appears to be unanswered. We have modelled for us prayers that are spoken, shouted and sung. We read of how prayer is silent. We see people praying using every part of their body as they stand, march, kneel and fall prostrate before the living God.

The Bible shows us the variety of prayer. We see prayers of worship and praise and thanksgiving; prayers that recognize sin and call out for mercy and forgiveness; prayers for our 'daily bread'; prayers of intercession, 'standing in the gap' and beseeching God on behalf of others. We are reminded that prayer is working in partnership with Father, Son and Holy Spirit for 'his kingdom to come and his will to be done on earth as it is in heaven'.

Down the centuries different traditions of praying using the Bible have arisen as Christians have grappled with the invitation to spend time with God in the place of prayer and all are in use today. For example, as we start to look into how the Bible informs our worship, we discover that most of the liturgy of long-established monasteries and convents and denominations is taken directly from the Bible.

One tradition, developed by Augustine of Hippo in the fourth century, involves God having a dialogue with us through Scripture. We transpose the written words directly into our present situation, as we allow the Holy Spirit to use our creative imagination and ask, 'What do these words mean for me here and now?'

We can taste the Bible, as we chew on the words of Scripture through *Lectio Divina* (sacred reading). This was developed by Benedict in the fourth century and then formalized into four steps by Guigo II in twelfth century. We start with reading the Word of God slowly over and over again a few times (*lectio*); and then reflect or meditate on it (*meditatio*). The third stage is responding to what it says through worship and prayer (*oratio*) before taking time to rest in God (*contemplatio*) staying open to how God is communicating and what he is leading us to do as an outcome.

We can explore the directive 'pray continually'

(1 Thessalonians 5:17) as many others have done in centuries past. By the sixth century the Jesus Prayer emerged in Eastern orthodoxy as a way of unceasing prayer: 'Lord Jesus Christ, Son of God, have mercy on me,' to use in time with the rhythm of breathing. Brother Lawrence sought to 'practice the presence of God' living his every waking moment in God's presence. Today we can memorize verses to meditate on or write our own breathing prayers.

We can look to discover the reality of God's presence revealed all around us by practically applying the living Word of God to our lives. As we read the text we ask the Holy Spirit to show us how he wants us to 'be' and what he wants us to 'do' through what we read. This form of praying arose out of the life of Francis of Assisi in the twelfth century.

We can use the knowledge we gain from reading and studying the Bible and pray from the text concentrating on the truth we discover. Our response in prayer as we ask the question, 'What does this text mean?' will be both emotional and intellectual, as developed by Thomas Aquinas in the thirteenth century.

We can enter into the Bible story and place ourselves into the original events described. As we do this the Scriptures can spring to life and we become a living part of them. This form of praying the Bible came from Ignatius Loyola in the fifteenth century and helps us to pray as we ask, 'What is God saying to me, now, through my direct involvement with this biblical story?'

And today new traditions of praying the Bible are evolving, for example praying the Lord's Prayer at noon or 'harp and bowl prayer', where sung worship and intercessory praying of Scripture are woven together following the models given in the book of Revelation. There are so many other ways to use the Bible to aid our praying, the challenge is: how will we respond to the challenge put to St John in the book of Revelation to 'take it and eat', allowing the Bible to inform and direct our prayers?

www.prayerforum.org   www.worldprayer.org.uk

 Jane Holloway is National Prayer Director for the World Prayer Centre and Director of the Prayer Forum of the British Isles and Ireland. She is author of *Prayer – A Beginner's Guide* (BRF, 2009).

IT CHANGED MY WORLD:

'I began to study the Bible five years ago, just after I became a Christian. I did not fully appreciate at the time what a blessing it was to be planted as a young Christian in such rich soil! As I have grown in my knowledge of God I have grown to love him more and I am passionate about telling others about his Word. I feel so thankful that God's Word has nurtured and grown me this far and I feel confident to stand on the truths he has revealed and look forward to seeing where he takes me next.' **Hannah**

NURTURED

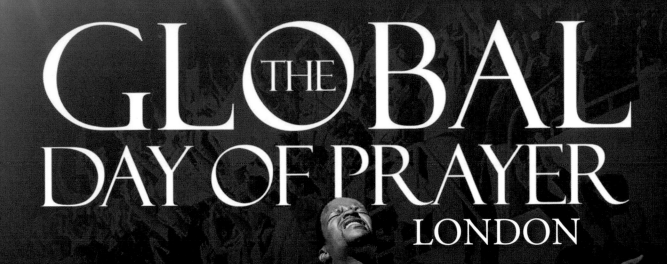

THE GLOBAL DAY OF PRAYER
LONDON

For Such a Time as This...

1 Million Praying the Lord's Prayer @ 12 noon

24 hour daily prayers across the Capital & Nation

Celebrating Pentecost in Unity

Calling the Nation to Wembley Stadium

Join this national prayer movement today
www.gdoplondon.com
08456 528 600

BOB HARTMAN

PLAYTIME!

The worst thing we can do is to treat the Bible too seriously. I'm serious. It's much too important for that.

The Pharisees played it that way. And it led them into a cul-de-sac of regulation and contorted interpretation and self-righteousness.

But Jesus played it differently. And I do mean 'played'.

With a wink and a smile, he opened up the Scriptures with stories about dodgy financial managers and impossibly large shrubbery. And the only contortions in his interpretation had to do with camels. And needles. And squeezing.

And speaking of squeezing, I think that if we squeeze anything too tightly, there's just the chance that we'll squeeze the life out of it. And that's what we sometimes do with the Bible.

So that's why we need to do what Jesus did with it. Particularly where our children are concerned. We need to play.

My grandmother loved to play. She was my Sunday school teacher, when I was in the Junior Boys class, and she was also a huge fan of those B-grade horror films – Boris Karloff and Bela Lugosi – you know the kind of thing. So when she told Bible stories to us, she told them like she was re-enacting *The Mummy*! Ehud, the judge, losing his left-handed sword in King Eglon's big belly. Athaliah, queen of Judah, murdering her own grandchildren to keep her throne. (Thanks for that, Grandma. I'll watch my back from now on!) Jezebel, devoured by dogs, except for the soles of her feet and the palms of her hands. (How did they manage that? I always wondered.) And most frightening of all, her rendition of The Plagues of Egypt, culminating with the dreaded question, 'And which of you boys are the firstborn in your family?'

The fact that I remember this, forty-odd years later, says

Look for the humour in the story.

everything. My grandmother loved those stories. She told them like she loved them. And she told them in a way that 9-, 10- and 11-year-old boys would appreciate. She was playing with them. And we just played along.

That's all storytelling is. A kind of playing. And if we play with these stories, and invite our children to play with us, I am convinced that all that is beautiful and challenging and funny and moving and transforming in these stories will open up for them.

How do we do that? We start by asking questions – questions about the story. That's what our kids do. It's just natural. Some of the questions will be answered by the text, itself: Who are the main characters? What is the setting? What is the problem that drives the story?

But some of the questions require a little imagination – a little play: Who else might have been there? What did that look like? Or smell like? Or feel like? And how would you have reacted, had you been there?

Those are all the questions I ask when I try to retell a Bible story. And, as I say, even if your kids don't ask them out loud, they are asking them in their heads. So why not ask them together?

Look for the humour in the story. That's the next thing. Everyone would rather laugh than cry. And there is so much in the Bible that's there to make us smile: Talking donkeys and hiding heroes and villains hoisted high on their own hanging machines! Think about it – the fact that Haman is so obsessed with having his revenge on Mordecai, that he builds a gallows in his own back garden is not only ultimately ironic, it's also hilarious! 'I'm popping down to B&Q, dear, for a few more two-by-fours and an extra strong length of rope. Oh, and sorry about the gnome.'

Playing is all about looking for those moments, and laughing about them together. Because, when we are laughing – when our eyes are wide open, when our mouths are wide open – then we are open, too. Open to whatever truth that story has for us. Playing is about holding the story lightly, letting it come to life on its own terms, not forcing it, not squeezing it. Letting it breathe.

I could happily recommend several volumes of biblical retellings that would help you do that. But I think the best way to tell a Bible story to the kids in your life, is to ask those questions yourself. Or, better still, to ask the questions with them. To find the humour, the life and the joy in those stories for yourselves. To discover what makes them 'shine' for you. And if you do that playfully, with a twinkle in the eye, with the sly grin, like I am convinced that Jesus did, someone will be remembering your retellings forty-odd years down the road as well. Because it will have helped them to fall in love with the stories, too.

Trust me. I'm serious.

Bob Hartman is a performance storyteller for children and author of numerous books, including *Best Mates* **(Authentic, 2009).**

BOB HARTMAN

THE TRICKSTER'S TALK

His attacker came from nowhere – out of the dark and the night. He grabbed Jacob round the waist and threw him to the ground.

Jacob tore himself free from his attacker and turned to face him. He expected to see a thief, or a madman, maybe. Or perhaps, even, his brother, Esau. But Jacob's attacker was none of those. He was bigger and stronger than any man that Jacob had ever seen. And there was something about him that had made Jacob wonder if he was even human!

Jacob knew he should run away, but there was something inside him that needed to go on wrestling. He had been wrestling all his life, it seemed. Wrestling with his father and his brother and his uncle, Laban. Wrestling to hold on to what he believed was his. And so he held on to his attacker as well – they wrestled all through the night!

'Who are you?' Jacob cried. 'What do you want?' But his attacker did not answer him. They grunted and struggled and rolled on the ground. And even when the attacker put Jacob's hip out of joint, Jacob did not let go. Finally, as the sun began to rise, Jacob's opponent spoke.

'Let me go!' he said. 'The sun is upon us.'

'No!' Jacob answered, struggling for breath. 'I will not let you go unless you give me something.'

'All right, then,' the opponent agreed. 'You will no longer be called Jacob – I will give you a new name. From now on you shall be known as 'Israel', for as the name suggests, you have struggled with God and persisted to the end!'

'Struggled with God?' Jacob wondered. 'But that must mean . . .' And so he asked. He had to ask. 'Then what is your name?'

Jacob's opponent smiled and said, 'I think you already know the answer to that question.'

And then he was gone!

Jacob fell to the ground and rubbed his aching hip. 'Could it be?' he wondered. Could it really be that he had seen the face of God, wrestled with the Almighty – and lived? And suddenly everything made sense – the whole of his long, wrestling life. God had a purpose for him. The struggles were all for a reason. To shape him and make him into the man, then the family, then the nation that God had promised to his father, Isaac, and his grandfather, Abraham.

And so Jacob rose and limped across the river, made peace with his brother Esau and returned to the land of promise. It looked as if everything would turn out all right.

But now . . . now Jacob's dream had become a nightmare. For Joseph, his special son, was dead. And all the struggling and wrestling had been for nothing.

Meanwhile, outside the tent, two of Jacob's other sons listened to him stirring and groaning.

'He's not taking it well,' one son observed.

'What did you expect?' shrugged the other. 'Joseph was his favourite.'

'Perhaps we should have told him the truth – that Joseph was sold into slavery.'

'What? And admit that we were the ones who did the selling? I don't think so, and besides, it's all quite fitting if you ask me. The old man got up to his fair share of tricks when he was our age. Now the last laugh is on him.'

Taken from *The Complete Bible Baddies* by Bob Hartman (Lion, 2005). Used by permission.

STORY OF THE MANGA BIBLE

MICHAEL NOVELLI

EXPLORING THE ART OF BIBLE STORYING

After 10 years in youth ministry, I felt as though I'd tried everything to help my students connect with the Bible. Then when an American missionary to Africa taught me the art of Bible storying, I realized it was more than just a new way to teach. It was a complete shift in how I could help students with their spiritual formation. It was about helping students become learners and observers of the Bible and life.

My experience with Bible storying over the past several years has changed everything about the way I look at my faith and ministry. Storying made such an impact on me that I now invest much of my time helping others discover this amazing new (yet ancient) way of experiencing the Bible.

What is Bible Storying?

Short for 'Chronological Bible Storying', storying is a sequential telling of Bible stories followed by a time of review and dialogue. This method is founded in the ancient Hebrew approach to the Scriptures – energetic storytelling, imaginative observation and lively dialogue.

Storying was introduced a few decades ago by missionaries who felt that understanding and teaching the Bible should not hinge on literacy. Recently, storying is also proving to be effective with youth and adults in media-literate, story-oriented western contexts.

The purpose of storying is to create an environment for us to discover and join in God's story. How do we create that environment? It is not easy . . . it requires us to cultivate an entirely new culture of learning, one where the expectations and responsibility of depth and discovery move onto the shoulders of the students. As leaders, our role is to foster an imaginative and inviting space for students to engage in a storytelling experience, creative retelling opportunities, and guided discussion.

What is the Bible Storying Process?

Here is one approach to Bible storying that I have found effective with my students:

1. Review of previous stories

This is a fast-paced and fun look back at stories you've already told. Use art and media – whatever you can – to help students reconnect. Review helps get everyone on up to speed and allows another opportunity for students to see connections between the stories.

2. Prepare for imaginative listening

We live in a culture of distraction. It is essential to the storying process that you set a reflective tone and challenge your group towards imaginative listening. Slow down, light a candle, and help your group concentrate so they can see the story unfolding in their minds.

3. Narrate the new story

This is where we tell the Bible story in a way that sparks imagination and brings it to life. I stitch together my own narratives from the Bible text in order to smooth out the language and make them more readable.

4. Replay the new story
The key to replaying is variety and fun. Use lots of different activities that will connect with different types of learners. Use art, drama, music – play and laugh together!

5. Dialogue about the story
Dialogue is where key truths emerge and the story starts to become 'our' story. Questions are used to direct students to discover insights from the stories. The goal is not for everyone to give the same answer – it is to spark wonder and careful observation of the story. In the midst of curiosity, connections and applications surface naturally. I use these kinds of questions to help spark thoughtful responses:

* Wondering questions to spark imaginative responses: 'When you listened to this story, what did you see in your mind?'
* Remembering questions to recount the details: 'How did this story describe God's relationship with Adam and Eve?'

6. Connection groups
Often I will break my students into smaller groups to process how the story is connecting with their own stories. This time will centre on discussion and prayer focused by a question like: 'You were created in God's image. How should this change the way you live?'

Bible storying is just one method of engaging with the Scriptures. Like any other, it has it strengths and weaknesses. Where it stands apart is that it gives students great opportunities to think for themselves, wonder, engage through multiple learning styles, and use reason and imagination congruently to enter the biblical story.

Bible storying is an adventure . . . it's a call to explore creative means, embarking on a new path of learning that asks a lot from our students and us. The reward of this adventure is great . . . a community of people transformed by God, ready to change the world. Together, may we find ourselves in the most amazing story ever told – God's story.

For further resources, training, and ideas about storying, go to www.echothestory.com

Michael Novelli leads youth ministries and serves youth workers by developing interactive resources and events to help students, educators and youth workers learn in new ways.

Taken from *Shaped by the Story: Helping Students Encounter God in a New Way* by Michael Novelli (Zondervan/YS, 2008). Used by permission.

•Bible Storying is an adventure . . . it's a call to explore creative means, embarking on a new path of learning

ADVENTURE

FRESHEN UP

10 BIBLE EXPERIENCE IDEAS

KRISH KANDIAH

Sometimes it takes a fresh experience of the Bible for us to gain an appetite for it again. I am hoping for a '*Lord of the Rings* factor' with the Bible Experience stream. Many people who went to see Peter Jackson's incredible production of the Tolkein's classic trilogy then went back to read the books. They wanted to see for themselves if Legolas really was supposed to snowboard down a rampart or if Éowyn really kills a Ringwraith. If we can provide our churches and our communities with experiences of the Bible, then we may, with God's help, witness a greater appetite for God and his Word in our lives.

Here are some ideas to help your church experience the Bible in a fresh way.

1. LIVING MUSEUM

The 400th anniversary of the King James Version of the Bible gives the church in the UK lots of opportunities. You could invite local schools into your church for a Bible exhibition or a living museum week. Resources such as the GLO Bible software could provide an instant high-tech interactive multimedia display if you have a couple of laptops and a data projector. Alternatively, members of the church could dress up and act in character so the children could meet Abraham, Moses or John the Baptist (a bit like in the film *Night at the Museum*).

2. THE MARK EXPERIENCE

This programme, developed in Southampton, helps the church take a weekend away to learn the whole of Mark's gospel. By enacting the whole gospel, participants get to experience the story in a brand new way, in all its intricacies and complexities.

3. ON THE STAGE

Why not invite a theatre company like Saltmine to come and do a performance of the Bible in your area? *Eden to Eternity* tells the whole Bible story in an hour, while the *God's Smuggler* production tells the exciting story of Brother Andrew. As you witness the lengths that Brother Andrew went to, to get Bibles into the former Soviet Union, it will make you value your own Bible much more.

4. GO NATURAL

I recently went on a lantern walk in some woodlands being run by A Rocha, a Christian conservation charity, which involved lots of stations with quizzes, hands-on nature exhibits, crafts and storytelling. It offered a great opportunity for Christians to demonstrate a concern for God's earth and a point of contact with the local community. Rural churches could run their own night walks with opportunities to tell the Bible story of creation – and new creation – as well as connecting with your environment and with your community.

5. FILM AND FAITH

A number of churches around the UK are using films as a point of contact, to help people encounter the Bible story. Almost any mainstream movie can be used for this: all you need is the correct licensing (a Churches Video License) available for most film companies from CCLI (www.ccli.co.uk). Alongside the pizza and popcorn, the film showing could be accompanied by a discussion about how the film either mirrors or contrasts with a biblical idea or story. Themes could vary from violence and self-sacrifice in Clint Eastwood's film *Gran Torino* to hope and friendship in *The Shawshank Redemption*. Alternatively you could compare and contrast the prodigal son story with *The Truman Show* or *Finding Nemo*. The important thing is that you are faithful to the intention of both the Bible and the film maker – not seeking to twist either to make your point. Watch out also for the film certificates and be upfront about strong language, violence or sexual content so that the audience knows what to expect. Several organizations, including Bible Society (www.reelissues.org.uk) and Damaris (www.damaris.org), produce resources to help the discussion to flow.

6. TRIPS AND TOURS

There are so many ways that the Bible has shaped our culture in the UK, which can be experienced through visits to all sorts of historic sites, museums and galleries. Churches can organize trips to places of historic and cultural interest and help people explore the connections between paintings, sculptures, monuments, significant buildings and the story of the Bible. Or you could be even more adventurous: I heard of one church that organized a sailing trip, which would not only have been a great day out, but would have provided plenty of illustrations for the gospel stories.

7. HUMMING AND STRUMMING

The Psalms were the staple of church worship gatherings for most of the 2,000 years of the church's lifespan. This could be a great year for us to rediscover the power of singing God's Word. Why not encourage the musicians in your church to set some of the Psalms to new tunes? You could even hold a songwriting competition and adopt the best entries into your regular worship.

8. ON LOCATION

Why not expose the church to something different, by filming the Sunday morning Bible reading on location each week? You could even ask those travelling abroad on holiday to film themselves while away, to add a global dimension! Particularly handy if they are visiting the Holy Land . . . Please do send us your YouTube links and we'll share them on the Biblefresh website.

9. GET YOUR HANDS DIRTY

For those more crafty among you, there are many ideas that can help you experience the Bible. Whether it's making unleavened bread at Passover, crafting cards with Bible verses at Christmas, or making pottery or writing on papyrus to get a feel for biblical times – you can let your imagination run wild!

10. PAINTING BY NUMBERS

Give artists within your congregation the freedom to paint depictions of the Bible passage during the service. As well as giving them time to prepare their materials, you may want to give them space to think and meditate on the passage in advance. At the end of the service, invite them to share their creation, with an explanation of how God spoke to them through the Bible passage. If you have several artists, you may end up with a gallery!

Krish Kandiah is Executive Director: Churches in Mission at the Evangelical Alliance and author of *Square Mile Workbook* (Authentic, 2009).

JOIN IN

3,300 churches
750 organisations
30 denominations

UNITING TO CHANGE SOCIETY

evangelical alliance
uniting to change society

Biblefresh is a JOINT initiative pioneered by the Evangelical Alliance. It is aimed at uniting organisations, churches and individuals in renewing their passion for the Bible.

www.eauk.org/joinin

NOTES

Welcome to Biblefresh

1 'Taking the pulse: is the Bible alive and well in the Church today?' (Bible Society)

A Guilty Secret

1 'Taking the pulse: is the Bible alive and well in the Church today?' (Bible Society)

An Atheist's Guide to the Gospels

1 Richard Dawkins, *The God Delusion*, (London: Bantam, 2006), p. 37-97.

2 William Lane Craig, 'Christ and Miracles' in *To Everyone An Answer: A Case for the Christian Worldview* (Downers Grove, IL: IVP, 2004), p. 142. cf. Francis J. Beckwith, 'Theism, Miracles, and the Modern Mind' in Paul Copan and Paul K. Moser (eds), *The Rationality of Theism* (London: Routledge, 2003); John Earman, *Hume's Abject Failure* (Oxford: Oxford University Press, 2000), R. Douglas Geivett and Gary R. Habermas (ed's), *In Defence of Miracles: A Comprehensive Case for God's Action In history* (Nottingham: Apollos, 1997).

3 Antony Flew with Roy Abraham Varghese, *There Is A God* (New York: HarperOne, 2007), p. 157.

4 Craig L. Blomberg, *The Historical Reliability of the Gospels*, second edition (Nottingham: Apollos, 2007), p. 251.

5 Antony Flew in Terry L. Miethe (ed.), *Did Jesus Rise From the Dead? The Resurrection Debate* (Eugene, OR: Wipf & Stock, 2003), p. 66.

6 Winfried Corduan, *No Doubt About It* (Nashville, TN: Broadman & Holman, 1997), p. 193.

7 Carsten Peter Thiede, *Jesus: Life or Legend?* (Oxford: Lion, 1990), p. 9.

8 J.P. Moreland, *Scaling the Secular City* (Grand Rapids, MI: Baker, 1987), p. 137. cf. Richard Bauckham, *Jesus and the Eyewitnesses: The Gospels as Eyewitness Testimony*, (Grand Rapids, MI: Eerdmans, 2006)

9 Walter A. Elwell and Robert W. Yarbrough, *Encountering the New Testament* (Grand Rapids, MI: Baker, 1998), p. 75.

10 Alister E. McGrath, *Jesus: Who He Is and Why He Matters* (Nottingham: IVP, 1994), p. 69.

11 Moreland, op cit, p. 148.

12 ibid, p.148-149.

13 ibid, p. 149.

14 cf. Dean L. Overman, *A Case for the Divinity of Jesus: Examining the Earliest Evidence* (Lanham, MD: Rowman & Littlefield, 2009)

15 ibid.

What About the Canon?

1 Alister McGrath, *Christian Theology: An Introduction*, 3rd ed. (Oxford: Blackwell, 2001) pp13-14

2 John Barton, *How the Bible Came to Be* (Louisville, KY: Westminster John Knox Press, 1998), p.85

3 F.F. Bruce, *The Books and Parchments: How we got our English Bible* (Basingstoke: Pickering and Inglis, 1984), p.117

Which Bible?

1 Nick Page, *The Longest Week*, (London: Hodder & Stoughton, 2009)

The Sequel?

1 N.T. Wright, *How can the Bible be Authoritative?* Originally published in *Vox Evangelica*, 1991, 21, 7-32.

2 Ibid.

3 Ibid.

But is it Art?

1 Quoted from his introduction to the *Pocket Canons Bible II: Psalms* (Edinburgh: Canongate, 1999)

And the Word Became Film

1 Matt Page lists 50 films about, or inspired by, Samson on his Bible Films blog (http://biblefilms.blogspot.com/2006/09/films-about-samson.html) though some like Samson vs. the Vampire Women have moved away from telling the biblical story!

The Holy Community at Table with Holy Scripture

1 James Houston gives an account of this 'energy and intelligence and prayer' in *The Act of Bible Reading*, ed. Elmer Dyck (Downers Grove, IL: InterVarsity Press, 1996), pp.148-73.

ACKNOWLEDGEMENTS

Compiled & edited by Alexandra Lilley
and Kim Walker

With thanks to Anna Moyle and
Andrew Horton.

Design and artwork by Mike Thorpe,
The Design Chapel
www.design-chapel.com

Illustrations by Simon AKA Vietnamthemovie
www.vietnamthemovie.co.uk and
Mike Thorpe

Photography by Rob Purbrick (London School
of Theology) and Mike Thorpe

Our thanks to all the contributors and to the
following organizations:

ABA Design
Authentic Media
Bible Society
Bible Society Wales
Centre for Biblical Literacy & Communication
Christianity Magazine
Churches for All
Cliff College
Collins
Damaris
Edmonton Baptist Church
Endis
Evangelical Alliance
Friends and Heroes
Hodder & Stoughton
Ichthus Christian Fellowship
IVP
Keswick Ministries
Lion Hudson
London Institute for Contemporary
Christianity
London School of Theology
The Methodist Church
Moorlands
Precept Ministries
Proclamation Trust
Prospects

Saltmine Trust
Scottish Bible Society
Share Jesus International
Soul Survivor
SPCK
Spring Harvest
St John's College, Durham
St John's College, Nottingham
St Mary's College, University of St Andrew's
Tearfund
Theos
Torch Trust for the Blind
Tyndale House
UCCF
Westminster Chapel
World Prayer Centre
Wycliffe Bible Translators
Zondervan

Grow with the Bible and the separate
organizations that they represent:
Bible Reading Fellowship
CWR
IBRA
Salvation Army
Scripture Union

We are grateful for the support and input
from the Biblefresh Bible Champions:

Ali Martin, Andy Croft, Andy Frost, Revd Dr Chris
Wright, Canon Dr Christina Baxter, Revd Colin Sinclair,
Revd Dave Burke, David Bradley, Revd David Jackman,
Revd David Meredith, David Miller, Revd Dr David
Wilkinson, Revd Gordon Kennedy, Revd Greg Haslam,
Prof. Howard Marshall, Dr Jamie Grant, Revd Jason
Clark, Jonathan Lamb, Rt Revd Lee Rayfield,
Revd Martin Allen, Martin Lee, Revd Dr Martyn Atkins,
Matt Summerfield, Michele Guinness, Revd Nims
Obunge, Dr Paula Gooder, Revd Richard Bewes,
Dr Robert Beckford, Rose Dowsett, Revd Simon
Downham, Revd Dr Simon Steer, Revd Stephen
Gaukroger, Revd Dr Steve Brady, Dr Steve Holmes,
Revd Stuart Bell, Terry Virgo, Bishop Tom Wright,
Dr Watcyn James.

www.biblefresh.com

15 14 13 12 11 10   7 6 5 4 3 2 1

First published 2010 by Authentic Media Ltd, Milton Keynes
www.authenticmedia.co.uk

Printed and bound in Great Britain by Bell & Bain Ltd., Glasgow

British Library Cataloguing in Publication Data

A catalogue record for this book is available from the British Library

ISBN: 978-1-86024-802-3